A Passion for Building
The Amateur Architect in England 1650–1850

AN EXHIBITION CURATED BY JOHN HARRIS AND ROBERT HRADSKY

SIR JOHN SOANE'S MUSEUM & NATIONAL TOUR

This exhibition, together with *Vaulting Ambition*, is supported by the M L A Designation Challenge Fund as part of the 'A Passion for Building' project. Both exhibitions will tour three regional UK venues during 2007–09.

With additional sponsorship from E Fuller & Son, Fullers (Builders) Ltd

A Passion for Building: the Amateur Architect in England 1650–1850
An exhibition at Sir John Soane's Museum, London, 18 May to 1 September 2007

Published in Great Britain 2007
by Sir John Soane's Museum

Reg. Charity No. 313609
www.soane.org

Text © Sir John Soane's Museum
Photographs © as indicated

ISBN 978-0-9549041-6-6

The Trustees of Sir John Soane's Museum would like to thank the benefactors, patrons and sponsors whose annual donations support the Museum's exhibition, education and conservation programmes.

PATRONS

Philip & Pamela Baldwin Bedlam Asset Management Sir William & Lady Benyon Anton & Lisa Bilton Peter Bloxham Remy Blumenfeld David & Molly Borthwick Richard Broyd Dominic & Sarah Caldecott Veronica Cohen Harriet Cullen Keith Day Mrs M Donald Paul Doyle Christopher Forbes Sir Rocco Forte William Fuller Richard & Claire Gapper Alison Gowman Veere Grenney Richard & Sheila Griffiths Richard Grigson Karl Grossfield Charles & Kaaren Hale Martin Halusa Philip & Linda Harley Christoph & Katrin Henkel Henryk Hetflaisz Philip Hewat-Jaboor David & Frances Hickman Ashley Hicks Michael Graham Hoare Richard Hoare Niall Hobhouse Stephen & Felice Hodges Carol Hogel Della Howard John & Rowena Jackson Danny and Gry Katz Pauline Karpidas James Kessler Laurence Kinney Norman Kurland George Laurence Victoria Legge-Bourke Oscar & Margaret Lewisohn Martin Lutyens Lulu and Charlie Lytle Sir Richard MacCormac Mallet, Lanto Synge Rick Mather Christopher & Henrietta McCall Katherine McCormick Joan Meyer Richard & Rosemary Millar Guy and Rose Monson Michael & Jan Moore John W Murray Sir Philip & Lady Naylor-Leyland Maureen & Francis Nicholls Amicia & Richard Oldfield Michael Palin William Parker James Perkins Lord & Lady Phillimore Olga Polizzi Claus & Valerie Prom Robin & Anne Purchas Lisbet Rausing & Peter Baldwin Janine Rensch Margaret & Tony Richardson Leopold de Rothschild Lily Safra Alex & Elinor Sainsbury Ian & Wendy Sampson Penny Shankar James & Shirley Sherwood Shaun Springer Oliver & Sally Stocken Alan & Ciannait Tait Chloe Teacher Andrew Templeton Britt Tidelius Bill & Suzie Tyne Fred & Kathy Uhde Robin Vousden Anthony Vernon Nicholas & Lavinia Wallop Peter & Marya Egerton-Warburton Richard White Michael and Jane Wilson

LIFE PATRONS
Debbie Brice The Hon. Elizabeth Cayzer Mirabel Cecil Deirdre J Hopkins Gisele Gledhill John & Virginia Murray Lord Rothschild

RECENT EXHIBITION SPONSORS
Savills and Sothebys *The Regency Country House: Photographs from the Country Life Picture Library*
The Henry Moore Foundation *Thomas Banks 1735–1805: Britain's First Modern Sculptor*
Lisbet Rausing and Peter Baldwin *Raymond Erith 1904–1973: Progressive Classicist*
J Paul Getty Charitable Trust *Saving Wotton: The Remarkable Story of a Soane Country House*
The Designation Challenge Fund *Hooked on Books: The Library of Sir John Soane, Architect 1753–1837*
The Heritage Lottery Fund *William West and the Regency Toy Theatre*
The Baring Foundation *'Architecture Unshackled': George Dance the Younger 1741–1825*
Howard de Walden Estates Limited *'Bob the Roman': Heroic Antiquity and the Architecture of Robert Adam*

For information on exhibition sponsorship and how to support the Museum as an individual Patron or through a company, trust or foundation please contact the Development Director: Mike Nicholson 020 7440 4241 or mnicholson@soane.org.uk

Sir John Soane's Museum, 13 Lincoln's Inn Fields, London WC2A 3BP Tel: 020 7405 2107 www.soane.org

Designed and typeset in Albertina by Libanus Press, Marlborough Printed by BAS Printers, Frome

Front cover: Detail of portrait of Theodore Jacobsen, architect of the Foundling Hospital, shown holding a drawing of the West Front, c.1742 by Thomas Hudson (1701–79) © Coram Family in the care of the Foundling Museum, London/Bridgeman Art Library
Back cover: Thomas Worsley, design for Hovingham Hall, Cat. 16
Title page: Thomas Worsley, design for a domed temple, Cat. 19
Opposite: Thomas Parkyns, anon. © National Portrait Gallery, London

CONTENTS

Foreword and Dedication 4

Some Thoughts on the Amateur intervention in English Architecture John Harris 5

Catalogue 25

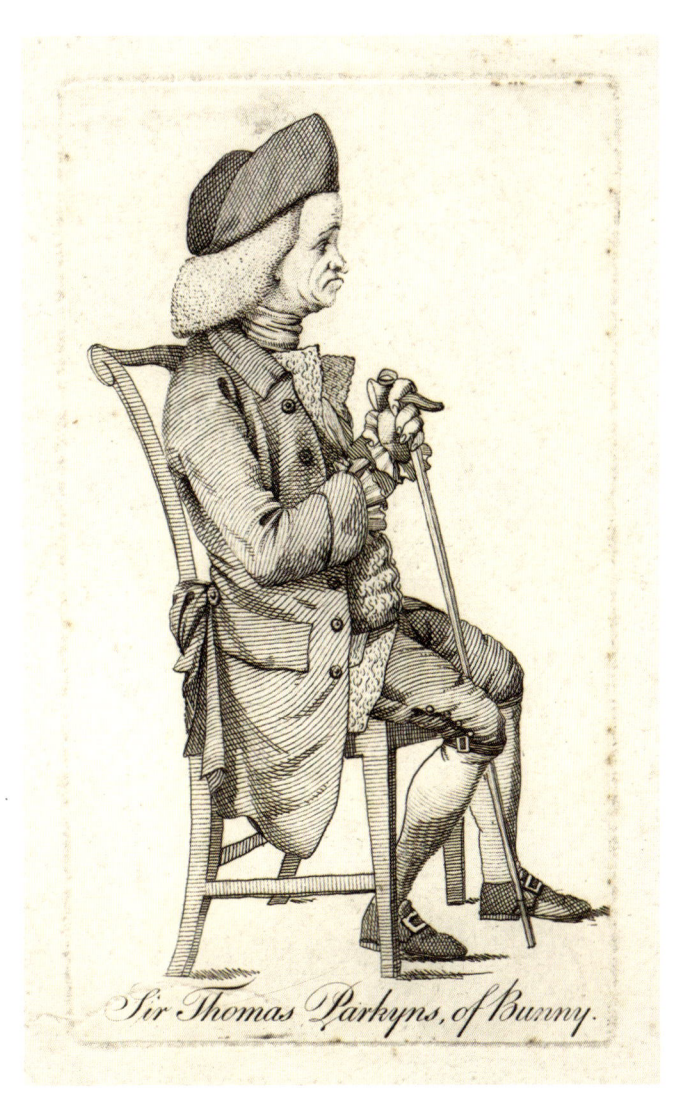

FOREWORD

Every professional architect must dread the interested amateur; the client who has read too many books and formed too many ideas. John Soane, who worked tirelessly to promote his profession and improve the training of architects, had many such opinionated clients. Unsurprisingly, the worst case of interference came during a government project, when a parliamentary campaign forced him, at a very late stage, to alter his design for the new Law Courts at Westminster from Palladian to Gothic.

Earlier in the 18th century, however, when the architectural profession was in its infancy, the amateur was king. An increase in foreign travel and a revival in the study of classical art and architecture inspired many landowning gentlemen to dabble in design. The resulting craze for DIY architecture, a phenomenon noted by foreign visitors, resulted in some of the most exciting and eccentric buildings in English architecture. And, as this exhibition shows, the amateur continued to make an impact deep into the 19th century – the church and Mausoleum built by Sarah Losh in the 1840s being but one glorious example.

This exhibition examines the work of a selection of amateurs between 1650 and 1850 and, in doing so, reveals a surprising diversity of building types and styles, as well as a host of colourful characters. More significantly, perhaps, it shows just how deeply the love of architecture and design penetrates the English psyche, and thus helps us to understand what drove a man like Soane to devote every waking hour to architecture.

I would like to thank the curators of this exhibition, John Harris and Robert Hradsky, who have approached this subject with a flare and enthusiasm very much in the spirit of the subject matter. I would also like to thank William Palin for organising the exhibition, Susan Palmer for overseeing the texts and Margaret Schuelein for her heroic efforts in conserving and mounting the many drawings on display.

This exhibition would not have been possible without the support of the lenders and sponsors. Of the former I would like to thank The Duke of Beaufort; The Syndics of Cambridge University Library; Sir Howard Colvin; Lord Daventry (Warwickshire County Record Office); Sir John and Lady Guinness; Hampshire Record Office; the National Trust; Tom North; Piers Pratt; the RIBA Drawings Collection; The Marquess of Salisbury; The National Archives of Scotland; Sir Edmund Verney and the staff at Claydon House, particularly Susan Ranson; West Yorkshire Archives; The Weston Park Foundation; Worcester College and Christ Church, Oxford; William Worsley and the Dean and Chapter of York.

Of the sponsors, the Museum is particularly grateful to the MLA Designation Challenge Fund for a substantial grant towards the origination of the exhibition and its tour to three regional venues. It is gratifying that the Soane Gallery will be merely the first stop in a tour covering some of the regions where amateur architects were most active.

TIM KNOX
Director, 2007

This exhibition was originated by Giles Worsley
1961–2006
and is dedicated to his memory

Some Thoughts on the Amateur Intervention in English Architecture

JOHN HARRIS

In 1755 J A Rouquet, a Swiss observer, could assert that 'in England more than in any other country, every man would fain be his own architect'. In this matter there can be no dispute, for England was unique in the possession of so many true amateurs. To show just how exclusively English this was, in Scotland one can name but a few, such as Alexander Fletcher, John Erskine, 11th Earl of Mar, Sir John and Sir James Clerk of Penicuick, or the Scottish expatriate the 7th Earl of Findlater in Dresden. In Europe there were the Renaissance amateur nobles or gentlemen such as Daniele Barbaro or Alessandro Tesauro, and later barely a dozen, that might include Frederick the Great, Gustav III of Sweden, Prince Leopold Friedrich Franz of Anhalt-Dessau, Conte Benedetto Innocente Alfieri, or maybe the Marquis de Voyer d'Argenson, the friend of Sir William Chambers, who described him as an 'Excellent Architect', though nothing is known of his designs. In contrast, a list of English amateurs documented between 1650 and 1850 easily adds up to more than seventy. However, there is a diversity of opinion as to what constitutes an amateur. So often the catalyst in England was the country house on its estate, in Sir Henry Wotton's words, 'an Epitome of the whole World', with the country house library as the nerve centre presided over by the landed gentleman with his classical education.

When the Georgian Group published their symposium, *The Role of the Amateur Architect*, in 1993 they provided alphabetical and chronological lists of 'amateur architects' that included such professionals as William Samwell, William Winde, Thomas Archer, Richard, 3rd Earl of Burlington, or William Wakefield. It is contended here that despite the fact that these belonged to the landed classes, they were architects practising as thorough professionals, all boasting a considerable body of work, and were not amateurs in the sense of Rees's definition of an amateur in his *Cyclopaedia* of 1803: 'Amateur is a foreign term introduced and now . . . current amongst us, to denote a person understanding and loving or practising the polite arts of painting, sculpture, or architecture without any regard to pecuniary advantage.' In the symposium Sir Howard Colvin observed that neither the word 'amateur', nor the word 'professional' is to be found in the eighteenth century. The Oxford English Dictionary gives an earliest date of 1784 for the word amateur. He concluded that those aristocrats and gentlemen who practised architecture might better be defined as Gentlemen Architects. In architecture Archer or Burlington practised as 'Gentlemen-Professionals', and even Sanderson Miller with more than 40 interventions, is dubiously an 'amateur'. Certainly in the case of Archer and Burlington a determinant as professional must surely be the establishment of an office with assistants or draughtsmen. Archer, as the designer of seventeen buildings, was as much a professional as Francis Smith with his busy family office in Warwick. He could hardly have built so much without some form of supervisory office. What Archer and his sort did not do, was to act as contractors or builders themselves.

This imprecise distinction in Britain between professional and amateur is bred of a lack of a state system of architectural training and education, common in Francophile Europe, based upon rigorous rules established by the French *Academie Royale d'Architecture* in 1671, where French architects were trained to serve the *Bâtiments du Roi*. However, what is shared by all architects, whether amateur or professional, is the need to learn to draw, as in 1726 when Thomas Worsley of Hovingham acquired William Salmon's *Polygraphice: or, the arts of drawing* (1701). As with Wren, so with Lord Burlington, a corpus of their designs shows an evolution in draughting competence from the smudgily washed-in presentation of a learner, to an ordered drawing where the wash is precisely contained within the outline drawing. By 1721, Burlington, the Architect Earl, was running an office with draughtsmen and a Clerk of Works, and the presentation designs are carefully drawn out by Henry Flitcroft. Burlington would hand over a rough plan or elevation with the instructions, 'I would have this drawn out fair by tomorrow morning.' At this point Burlington is no amateur. He is as competent as all the professionals he effectively nurtured in his office and sent out to official appointments. Sir James Clerk (1709–83) of Penicuick House, Midlothian, a Scottish amateur who made many designs for his own house at

Penicuick, 1761–69, in praising 'gentlemanly commitment', thought that Burlington 'gloried more in the title of Architect than of his peerage', which was also the opinion of Lord Chesterfield, when he wrote to his son on 17 October, 1749, 'You may soon be acquainted with the considerable parts of civil architecture; and for the minute and mechanical parts of it, leave them to masons, bricklayers and Lord Burlington; who has, to a certain degree, lessened himself by knowing them too well.' But there was something else that puts Burlington in a quite different category from other gentlemanly amateurs: his crusading belief that his role was to change architectural taste, a task that he had clearly discussed with William Kent in Italy as early as 1719.

Both Maurice Howard and Mark Girouard have dealt with the building process and the Elizabethan patron, observing that the involvement of a Sir William Cecil of Burghley, Northamptonshire, or a Sir Thomas Smyth of Hill Hall, Essex, in building was not amateur intervention as in the eighteenth century. Girouard warns against identifying Surveyors of the Royal Works under Elizabeth I as architects in our sense of the definition, observing that courtier patrons were not dealing with 'architects of authority and repute but with comparatively uneducated and obscure artificers'. There is evidence that Cecil involved himself in annotating plans of Theobalds following his acquisition of that estate in 1564, and possessed in his library at Burghley, Androuet du Cerceau's 1559 *Livre d'architecture* and Philibert de l'Orme's 1561 *Nouvelles inventions pour bien bastir*, as did Sir Thomas Smyth, whose library contained a section on 'Architectura'. Sir Christopher Hatton of Holdenby in Northamptonshire possessed two copies of Palladio, and Grace Cavendish, Bess of Hardwick's daughter-in-law, signed the first edition of Palladio's *I Quattro Libri* soon after its publication in 1570. The 'Wizard' Earl of Northumberland at Petworth House, Sussex, owned a distinguished architectural library, as did Sir Francis Willoughby of Wollaton Hall, Nottinghamshire. This suggests gentlemanly intervention, but there was rarely a continuity of cause and effect as might occur when a Georgian gentleman architect involved himself in the building of his house. Elizabethan courtiers were frequently away from their houses for long periods, absences that resulted in lack of surveillance and changes of plans.

However, there is one project that can be dated to between 1605 and 1610, Jacobean rather than Elizabethan, perfectly fulfilling the criteria for an Elizabethan gentleman architect. Nothing like it would appear in English architecture until the mature Inigo Jones. It stands alone in Britain as a pure Vitruvian example of the classical revival. The author was Sir John Osborne (c.1550–1628) of Chicksands Priory in Bedfordshire, his design a 'Porticus', or two-storey loggia or colonnaded building with superimposed porticoes facing outwards at each end, the whole a viewing or parading platform fronting the Thames at the Strand palace of Robert Cecil, Earl of Salisbury. The elevation conforms to Osborne's written specification, and the proportions were Vitruvian, Osborne using editions of Vitruvius and Serlio as well as Vredeman de Vries's *Architectura oder Bauung der Antiquen aus dem Vitruvius* of 1577. How we would love to be able to peer into Osborne's library. What enriches this discovery is the association of the design of the 'Porticus' with the making of the Haynes Grange Room, whose panelling is now in the Victoria and Albert Museum, which may well have originated around 1610 as the Pigeon Gallery in Osborne's Chicksands Priory, to which Haynes Grange was a hunting lodge.

The gentleman architect as we define the term is really a phenomenon of post-Restoration in 1660, and the era of the enquiring Royal Society. The arch architectural gentleman designer was Sir Roger Pratt (1620–85), who had spent six years of exile on the Continent studying the 'best authors of Architecture', returning in 1649 with many notebooks, clearly intended for a treatise on architecture,

Sir Roger Pratt by Sir Peter Lely (1618–80), c.1680 Private Collection

Above: Weston Park, Shropshire, south front © The Weston Park Foundation
Below: Elizabeth, Lady Wilbraham by Sir Peter Lely (1618–80), *c.*1670 © The Weston Park Foundation/ The Bridgeman Art Library

including practical 'Rules for the Guidance of Architects' and 'Notes on the Building of Country Houses', in which he offers advice to those gentlemen contemplating building. He advises the prospective builder 'to resolve with yourself what house will be answerable to your purse and estate. Then if you be not able to handsomely contrive it yourself, get some ingenious gentleman who has seen much of that kind abroad and been somewhat versed in the best authors of Architecture: viz. Palladio, Scamozzi, Serlio etc. to do it for you, and to give you a design for it on paper.' Pratt did more than any other professional architect to change architectural taste, for following the completion of the Jonesian Coleshill, Berkshire, in 1662 for his uncle Sir George Pratt, there followed three magisterial houses: in 1663–65, Kingston Lacy, Dorset, for Sir Ralph Bankes, and Horseheath Hall, Cambridgeshire, for William, Lord Alington; and in 1664–67 Clarendon House, Piccadilly, for Edward Hyde, 1st Earl of Clarendon, this last, in the words of Howard Colvin, 'one of the most influential buildings in the history of English domestic architecture'. Pratt's elevation for Kingston Lacy is competently drawn and presented, and there is no reason to doubt that it is in his hand. He was familiar with professionals such as Hugh May and Sir Christopher Wren, and with those connoisseurs versed in architecture such as John Evelyn, who himself merits inclusion in Colvin's *A Biographical Dictionary of British Architects* by virtue of his role as a virtuoso and the author of the English edition of Roland Fréart's *Parallèle de l'Architecture antique et de la moderne*, 1650, in 1664. However, it is difficult to identify any building designed by him. So often in the case of Pratt and other like gentlemen, knowledge and expertise was conveyed conversationally.

Pratt's notebooks are exceptional, but they do not indicate how he supervised the building process, if in fact he did. The building of four major houses in the space of six years, all of high quality, would suggest close supervision on his part, but his executants are not known. There is a similar lack of information about Lady Wilbraham, born Elizabeth Mytton, to whom has been attributed the building of Weston Hall, Staffordshire, in 1671, and Woodhey Hall and the Woodhey Chapel, Cheshire, *c.*1690. Evidence for the architectural skills of this lady rests

upon her extensive notes and memoranda in her copy of Godfrey Richards's *The First Book of Architecture by Andrea Palladio* in the 1663 English edition. So familiar was she with the technical and practical aspects of building, that she has been given the role of amateur architect. However, any attribution to her of the whole designing process must proceed with caution, for there was surely an executant, who may have been William Taylor, a London-based architect of some importance, who was at Weston in 1674.

Roger North (?1653–1734) belonged to the same scientific circles as John Evelyn. A learned connoisseur rather than practitioner of architecture, he learnt much from Fréart, particularly 'most clear instruction . . . and . . . a clear notion of the five orders'. North was called to the Bar in 1675. In 1683 he became Treasurer of Middle Temple and, having tasted for the first time 'the joys of designing and executing' architecture built the imposing Gateway on Fleet Street (completed in 1684). This severe elevation with minimal ornament reflects North's opinion, in his unpublished *Essay on Building*, that Inigo Jones designed 'all things well and great'. This delight in plain structures was expressed in his own house at Rougham in Norfolk, where through the 1690s he raised a new wing with an astonishingly precocious four-column Ionic portico with a mid-way gallery based upon Palladio's Villa Sarego in the *Quattro Libri*. Surprisingly, North's praise of Jones can be matched at this time from Paris, where in 1698 the Earl of Portland reported the recollections of a M. d'Auzot after viewing the Banqueting House, 'that it was preferable to all the Buildings on this side of the Alps', affirming that 'Inigo Jones, the Architect, had a true relish of what was noble in that art.' This early move to reassess Jones may first emanate from Oxford, but with Scottish connections.

THE OXFORD CIRCLE

In Oxford Henry Aldrich (1648–1710) succeeded to the office of Dean of Christ Church in 1689, and served as Vice-Chancellor of the University from 1692 to 1695. Significantly he was tutor to Sir Andrew Fountaine, and later in 1705, to Henry, Lord Herbert, later 9th Earl of Pembroke, two amateurs who would be closely linked both in friendship and architecture. Alas that Aldrich's will instructed the destruction of his personal papers, for these would have enlightened us about his travels and architectural activities. Music, heraldry, mathematics, logic, Greek and Latin texts, antiquities – all were part of his remit. He possessed one of

Mezzotint of Henry Aldrich by John Smith, after Sir Godfrey Kneller (1646–1723), 1699 © National Portrait Gallery, London

the finest private collections of books on antiquities, and is believed to have spent a 'considerable time' in Italy, where he discoursed with the 'eminent in architecture'. His was clearly a powerful influence, as is shown by the direction of Sir Edward Hannes, when bequeathing in 1710 £1,000 to the building of the Westminster School Dormitory, that both Wren and Aldrich should be consulted in the 'contriving'. Although he advised on many Oxford buildings as one of the university's 'able judges of architecture', only the Peckwater Quadrangle at Christ Church begun in 1706, can unequivocally be his, although the design of All Saints Church, as in the engraving by Michael Burghers in 1701, is probably his. The Peckwater Quadrangle, strongly Jonesian in composition, is one of the forerunners of neo-Palladian urban design, anticipating Colen Campbell's designs for Grosvenor Square, London, 1725, and John Wood's for Queen Square, Bath, 1729. At some point before his death Aldrich was compiling an *Elementa Architecturae Civilis*, a Vitruvian treatise devoted to 'Civil and Military Architecture', of which only ten copies of the first 44 pages were printed in his lifetime. His significant contribution was the authority he brought to bear on the study of architecture and antiquity, and his knowledge of this may well have influenced Nicholas Hawksmoor's many Oxford works. It was Aldrich who persuaded Charles Fairfax to undertake the Latin translation of Palladio's *Antichità di Roma*, published in 1709, where in the preface Fairfax states that Palladio was Aldrich's 'professed master in architecture'. In Aldrich's collection of drawings was his copy of the Teatro Olympico drawn by John Webb, and it is reasonable to believe that Aldrich thought this to have been drawn by Jones. It is still a mystery where Aldrich acquired his mastery of architectural draughtsmanship, demonstrated by the drawings for the *Elementa Architecturae Civilis*, now in Worcester College Library, or by his unexecuted Palladian design for the north side of the North Quadrangle at All Souls College, c.1710, also at Worcester College.

Towards the end of Aldrich's life Dr George Clarke (1661–1736) emerged to take his place as an Oxford virtuoso and man of taste playing a similar role in the university's architectural patronage. Among many projects, at his own college of All Souls he designed the Warden's Lodging in 1706; from the year of Aldrich's death in 1710 he was consulted over the Clarendon Building; in 1716 he revised Aldrich's design for the south side of the Peckwater Quadrangle; from 1710 to 1721 he was working with Hawksmoor at Queen's College; and one of his last works was to propose a design for extended wings to Worcester College. Among his sketches at Worcester College is an elevation of a neo-Palladian porticoed villa, inscribed by Clarke, 'Ld Ranelagh's'. It can only be a project for converting the brick Wrennian house by Chelsea Hospital, designed and built c.1688-89 by the 1st Earl of Ranelagh, into a Palladian villa by the Thames. This could be a prescient design by Clarke, but it might have been made by Ranelagh himself before his death in 1712. As Colvin aptly comments on Clarke, 'As a draughtsman he was clumsy and inelegant, but could convey an architectural idea to paper well enough to make it comprehensible, and when the need arose he could rely on Hawksmoor and Townesend to act as his architectural amanuenses and interpreters.'

Aldrich as an innovator can hardly have ignored Dr David Gregory (1661–1708), another Oxford enthusiast for architecture who would also have known Clarke. In February 1699 Gregory was corresponding with Alexander Fletcher of Saltoun Hall, East Lothian, about Fletcher's designs for a small house based upon a cube. This design is astonishing, a windowed elevation of alternate triangular and segmental pediments with voussoired windows to the basement. It would not look out of place if presented as by James Gibbs in 1715, or indeed, and more relevantly, as by Colen Campbell, for Fletcher places his stairs squarely in the centre of the house, as did Campbell at Shawfield in 1710. Gregory and Fletcher are again in correspondence on 21 April 1707, thus implying eight years of interest in architecture, about the construction of a Tuscan roof as at St Paul's Covent Garden, Gregory commenting that Hawksmoor was the only person he knew who had made drawings of that church. All this must surely be an extension of Aldrich's interests. But it is more than that, for Fletcher might well belong to a circle that would include Campbell's master, the architect James Smith, in this shadowy period when Campbell the lawyer was emerging amateur-like into Campbell the professional architect.

AN OXFORD LEGACY

Campbell was involved in the early years of the architectural career of Henry, Lord Herbert (c.1689–1750, from 1733 the 9th Earl of Pembroke), who had matriculated from Aldrich's tuition at Christ Church in 1705 and is reported in Venice in 1712. At what point Herbert turns to architecture is uncertain, but as these gentleman architects had to have an amanuensis, Herbert's may have initially been Campbell, who in 1719 may have discovered the young Roger Morris at Sir Andrew Fountaine's Narford Hall. In

The Palladian Bridge at Wilton © Crown copyright.NMR

1724 the Campbell–Morris duo was involved in the building of the Countess of Suffolk's Marble Hill, Twickenham, and Herbert's own Pembroke House, Whitehall, two early buildings by Herbert. Herbert is among the few amateur architects who could claim many buildings due to his intervention, most notably c.1730 his own Westcombe House, Kent, and the Water House at Houghton Hall, not far from Narford; in 1732 the Duchess of Marlborough's Wimbledon House, Surrey, and in 1736 the exquisite Palladian Bridge at his beloved Wilton. To quote George Vertue when describing the Palladian Bridge a few years after its completion, all Pembroke's works were 'built by his direction'. The 'purity of his architectural taste' is apparent in all of these.

There are many Pembrokian connections that need scrutiny. One in particular is intriguing. That other gentleman architect who was taught by Doctor Aldrich was Sir Andrew Fountaine (1676–1753), who succeeded to the family estate at Narford in Norfolk in 1706, where the house had probably been built 1702–04 by Henry Bell of Kings Lynn, one of those 'amateurs', in this case a Lynn merchant, who were really professionals. Fountaine's library was impressive, almost solely devoted to architecture and antiquity, with more than 42 titles of treatises. As Vice-Chamberlain to Caroline, Princess of Wales, not only can Fountaine be identified with a group of patrons who employed Campbell, but he was also on friendly terms with Lord Burlington, who wrote to him about architecture from Italy in 1719. When Burlington decided to replace his baroque paintings by Antonio Pellegrini in Burlington House by more classicizing ones by Sebastiano Ricci, he gave the Pellegrini canvasses to Fountaine, where they were adapted for the hall at Narford. Both William Halfpenny in his *Art of Sound Building* in 1725 and Robert Morris in his *Essay in Defence of Ancient Architecture*, 1728, couple Fountaine's name with Burlington and Pembroke as 'practitioners' of [Palladian] architecture. Fountaine laid out a garden at Narford in the antique manner, published in 1725 by Campbell in the third volume of *Vitruvius Britannicus*, but intended for the second volume in 1717, a vital clue to elucidating Narford's dating. No garden was as influential upon the future Chiswick, and c.1717 accords well with the tradition that in 1719 Fountaine extended his house by a courtyard range that included a library with a frontal astylar elevation and flanking elevations that were entirely in Campbell's style. Campbell could have been Fountaine's executant, and it is not impossible that he, Campbell and Morris were all here together at some time. Indeed in the 1730s Pembroke was advising Fountaine on interior décor at Narford, employing Andien de Clermont, his and Morris's favourite decorator, for ceilings in the antique Roman manner.

THE YORKSHIRE CONNECTION

Both Pembroke and Burlington, as Architect Earls, figure in the achievements of Sir Thomas Robinson (c.1702–77), that other gentleman architect designing professionally, whose Plinean Antique-Roman villa at his own Rokeby in Yorkshire can almost stand comparison with Burlington's Chiswick. Robinson's intention to build can be dated to 1724 when he rejected a Baroque design by the Yorkshire architect William Wakefield, and within a year had resolved to be his own architect. Rokeby's gardens were also Antique in conception, influenced by Robert Castell's folio on the *Villas of the Ancients Illustrated*, 1729. Rokeby stands in a sequence of Yorkshire buildings by amateurs that lead to Thomas Worsley's Hovingham, and on to Lord Grantham, and ultimately to Earl de Grey, Yorkshire in origin, but busy rebuilding Wrest Park, Bedfordshire. A set of engravings of Rokeby are signed 'T. Robinson Bar. Architectus', and may have been drawn by Isaac Ware, who

Sir Thomas Robinson, by Frans van der Mijn (1719–83), 1750
© National Portrait Gallery, London

Rokeby Park, south front © Mortham Estates (Trustee) Ltd

may have served periodically as Robinson's amanuensis. Robinson's design for Rokeby church was drawn by Ware for engraving, although the church was not completed until 1776. But much is speculation, and it is uncertain how Robinson functioned, for he developed an extensive practice after he returned from the Governorship of Barbados in 1747. This included a new western wing for Lord Carlisle, his father-in-law, at Castle Howard, Yorkshire in 1753; Prospect Place, a large house for himself on the Thames at Ranelagh Gardens, where he was Master of Ceremonies in the 1750s; a Gothic Gateway for Richard Trevor, Bishop of Durham, at Bishop Auckland Castle, Co. Durham, in 1760; and Trevor's Glynde church, Sussex, in 1763, after a design by Robert Hampden Trevor in the form of interlocking hexagons had been rejected. At his death in 1777 he was building a huge house at Claydon, Buckinghamshire, for the 2nd Earl Verney. He is central to a group of Yorkshire architects, both amateur and professional. Perhaps he did receive some pecuniary advantage, so strapped was he always for cash.

Burlington was also a Yorkshire landowner, whose family seat was Londesborough Hall. He too belongs to this northern coterie by virtue of his frequent visits there, and for his design for the York Assembly Rooms in 1731, and his involvement with Roger Morris in the building of Kirby Hall for Stephen Thompson in the years after 1747. The web of connections is complex. Burlington was a friend of Colonel James Moyser (c.1688–1751), who lived at Beverley, designed Bretton Hall for Sir William Wentworth about 1730, and provided designs for Nostell Priory from as early as 1731. Even if posthumously, Campbell is an *éminence grise* at Nostell, for a design by him prefigures the house as built from 1737, its plan based upon Palladio's Villa Mocenigo. Campbell must have known both the father and son Moysers. He designed Sir Charles Hotham's house in Eastgate, Beverley, in 1716, William Thompson's Ebberston Lodge, in 1718, Sir William Robinson's Newby (now Baldersby) Park, in 1720, and for John Aislabie, Lady Robinson's brother, at Studley Royal, with Morris at his side, shortly before he died in 1729.

The death of Robinson of Rokeby in 1777 neatly coincides with that of Thomas Worsley (1711–78), who in 1750 had succeeded his father at Hovingham Hall, Yorkshire. There is internecine amateur endeavour here, for Worsley's sister Frances married Sir Thomas Robinson of Newby, who had succeeded as 2nd Baron Grantham in 1770. Far more significant in this matter of family relationships, providing evidence for Worsley's architectural education, is the fact that his mother Mary was the daughter of Sir Thomas Frankland, 3rd Baronet (c.1685–1747), of Thirkleby Park, barely 12 miles from Hovingham. It has never been

Hovingham Hall, view from south-west

Hovingham Hall, view towards the village through the entrance to the riding school
Country Life Picture Library

observed that in the house was one of the most notable architectural libraries in England. Sir Thomas Frankland, the 2nd Baronet (1665–1726), is only known for his patronage of Nicholas Hawksmoor, who made unexecuted designs for stables in 1704, and may have designed the church, now demolished. The library was dispersed in London at the 3rd Baronet's death by Samuel Baker, 18–19 June 1747. Out of 200 titles, more than 70 are architectural, covering all the Italian and French treatises, so standing comparison with Burlington's own library. It would beggar belief that Worsley did not use the Thirkleby as his school of architecture.

Worsley's interest in architecture can be taken back to his schooling at Eton, where he inscribed William Salmon's *Polygraphice: or, the arts of drawing*, 1701, 'T Worsley 1722 ex libris'. In 1728 he drew there a Doric order that he inscribed 'T W Etonensis 1728'.

Worsley's interests were divided between his skill with the horse and his love for architecture. Both were combined when he was appointed in 1760 by George III, no doubt through his close friendship with John, 3rd Earl of Bute, to the sinecure of the Surveyorship of the Works, in other words the political boss of Henry Flitcroft, then the Comptroller of the Works, and of William Chambers and Robert Adam, the joint Architects to the King. Worsley also involved himself in matters concerning the king's horses, in particular the designing of the King's Riding School at Buckingham House. However, Worsley's architectural ambitions had begun much earlier than the royal appointment, for about 1740 he had designed stables for John Hutton at Marske Hall, Yorkshire, and by the mid-1750s had begun building a new house at Hovingham. Just as with his service to the king, so at Hovingham he combined architecture with his horses, taking as his starting point the Roman House as reconstructed by Palladio, giving stables and *manège* pride of place with the dining room and saloon, wrapping them around with conventional Palladian elevations. Towards this end he made many designs, still in family possession at Hovingham, where the collection includes a great number by officers of the King's Works, no doubt purloined by Worsley to serve as exemplars.

Continuing family relationships in this Yorkshire Connection, Thomas Worsley's nephew, Thomas Robinson (1738–86), was also infected with the architectural mania. He had been sent on the Grand Tour from 1758 to 1760, returning with architectural interests learnt in the Turin Academy, where Lord Newborough, another amateur, was a student with him. Upon Robinson's succession as 2nd Baron Grantham in 1770 he was sent to Madrid as Ambassador from 1771 to 1779, from where his correspondence with Sir William Chambers is full of architectural matters. Whether his ability as an architectural designer was related to Thomas Worsley's interests is not known. His was a very attractive draughtsmanship, as shown by his design for a tower for his brother-in-law John Parker at Boringdon House or Saltram House, Devon, or his charming design for a Rustic Hut at his Baldersby, or a Triumphal Arch proposed for Hyde Park Corner in 1761. In 1780 he married Mary Jemima, the second daughter of Philip, 2nd Earl of Hardwick. Their son Thomas Philip (1781–1859) succeeded as 3rd Baron Grantham in 1786 aged five. In 1803 by changing his name to Weddell, he inherited from William Weddell the family seat of Newby Hall, so confusingly becoming the owner of two seats of the same name. Upon inheriting the title of Earl de Grey and Baron Lucas in 1833 through his mother, he changed his name again. As Weddell he had designed the dining-room to Newby in 1808, and in 1834, now as the master of Wrest Park, Bedfordshire, he began the total rebuilding of this great English house, replacing it with a chateau in a French Louis XV style, aptly described by Howard Colvin as a '*tour de force* of French eighteenth-century architectural design on English soil carried out with consistent skill both inside and out', the result of de Grey's many visits to Paris. He had clearly inherited the family's architectural genes. De Grey writes, 'I was strictly and in every sense of the word my own architect ... I had my French books always under my hand [and] referred to them for authority whenever I could find anything to suit me.' His executant was James Clephan, who had been Clerk of Works from 1815 at Ravensworth Castle, Durham, and from 1831 at Barrington Park, Berkshire, both houses designed by another amateur, Thomas Liddell, the son of the 1st Lord Ravensworth. The French books consulted by de Grey are symbolically represented on spines over the south door of the entrance hall of Wrest: 'Blondel', 'Mansard', 'Le Pautre', and the south front of the house is based upon a model in Blondel's *Maisons de Plaisir*. De Grey was also responsible for the design of the Silsoe Lodges in 1826 and Silsoe Church in 1830–31. He was chairman of the building committee for the United Services Club in Pall Mall in 1827, a member of the commission to superintend the building of Edward Blore's entrance front of Buckingham Palace in 1847, and in 1848 a representative on the Royal Commission to rebuild the new Houses of Parliament. From 1835 until his death in 1859 he served as the first President of the Royal Institute of British Architects.

AMATEUR ARCHITECTS & PROFESSIONAL EXECUTANTS

The role of the executant is perfectly demonstrated by the amateur designs of Theodore Jacobsen (died 1772), a merchant who managed the City operations of the Hanseatic Steelyard. He shared a busy commercial career with designing architecture, always requiring an executant. For the East India Company House in Leadenhall Street in 1726 John James was his builder. This commission may have encouraged the Bank of England in the same street to consider Jacobsen's design, later engraved, for the new Bank in 1731, but preferred that of its surveyor George Sampson. Between 1742 and 1752 Jacobsen designed his most ambitious work, the Foundling Hospital,

Theodore Jacobsen, holding a drawing of the west front of the Foundling Hospital, by Thomas Hudson (1701–79), c.1742
© Coram Family in the care of the Foundling Museum, London/ The Bridgeman Art Library

Chalk sketch of Thomas Philip de Grey, 2nd Earl de Grey (detail), by Sir George Hayter (1792–1871) c.1820 © National Portrait Gallery, London

St John the Evangelist, Wicken, Northamptonshire, plaster vaulting over chancel   English Heritage.NMR

a remarkable essay in astylism, the execution of which was entrusted to James Horne, who also built Jacobsen's Royal Naval Hospital at Haslar near Portsmouth, designed in 1745, but not completed until 1761. At Trinity College, Dublin, Horne was again the executant for Jacobsen of the main quadrangle between 1752 and 1759, where John Sanderson, an executant for other amateurs, also provided advice. When George Vertue dined with Jacobsen at Lonesome Lodge, Wooton, Surrey, in 1747, he commented that the house 'was of his own design [1740] and building'. At Jacobsen's death his will refers to a portfolio of his designs and copperplates, including the Triangular House, the Bank of England, and the Foundling Hospital. He composed in a plain unassuming Palladian style, the Foundling Hospital and the Royal Naval Hospital planned as linked pavilions around a courtyard.

It is very likely that Robert Dingley (1710–81), a member of the Russia Company, Director of the Bank of England, and Governor of the Foundling Hospital, knew Jacobsen well. He too had Yorkshire connections for his first wife was Elizabeth, the daughter of Henry Thompson of Kirby Hall. However, as far as we know all Dingley's architectural designs are paper inventions: for the Magdalen Hospital in Surrey, c.1763, for the engraved rustic temples at West Wycombe Park, Buckinghamshire, and for the King's and Queen's Baths at Bath soon after 1766. Only in Yorkshire in 1754 does he appear on a site when involved in the building of John Carr's Knavesmire Race Stand, presumably due to his Yorkshire interests.

John Sanderson (died 1774) seems to have been the chosen executant of many amateurs. Thomas Prowse (c.1708–67) employed him in 1753 to build the remarkable fan-vaulted Wicken church, Northamptonshire, on the estate of his wife. In the same year he was assisting Prowse, and that other amateur, Sir Roger Newdigate, in their design for John Conyers's Copped Hall, Essex. In 1754 he aided Sanderson Miller to draw out plans 'properly figured for the direction of the workmen', at the Palladian tower house at Hagley Hall, Worcestershire, and he was probably the executant in 1755 of Prowse's designs for John Collins at Hatch Court, Somerset, the year he was involved in the interior remodelling of Kimberley Hall, Norfolk, where the four Palladian towers were 'fix'd by Prowse's just palladian hand', and the interiors were in Sanderson's rococo style.

THE GOTHICISTS

The Gothic Revival in the eighteenth century is complicated by virtue of a sort of no man's land between Gothic survival and revival. Parsons were educated men who must have often figured out a Gothic alteration to a church. It was quite a different matter with the emergence of the Georgian antiquary. In 1717 the newly founded Society of Antiquaries voted John Talman (1677–1726) its first Director and William Stukeley (1687–1765) its Secretary. Talman was not an amateur in our sense of the word, for he might almost have been described as a professional antiquary. His designs for the Hall and Chapel of All Souls, Oxford, offered in March 1708, self-confessedly 'unlike any other in Oxon & pretty much after ye Italian Gothic', occupy a unique place in the Gothic Revival, as indeed, does John Freeman's Gothic building, that may well have been composed in the late 1720s. Stukeley and Talman were partners in antiquarian enquiry until the latter's death in 1726. In the 1740s Stukeley had been befriended by John, 2nd Duke of Montagu, who shared with him 'exactly the same taste for old family concerns, genealogy, pictures, furniture, coats of arms, the old way of building, gardening and the like; in a general imitation of pure nature in the Gothic architecture, in painted glass, in the open hearted, candid way in designing and free manner of conversation', in which Montagu had a 'very good knack of drawing and designing'. Stukeley designed a Gothic Bridge for the park at Boughton, Northamptonshire, in 1744, and his unexecuted design for a chapel in the north-east wing of Boughton is a most daring and precocious Gothic fan-vaulted space that has no precedent in the Revival. This 'free manner of conversation' was peculiar to the construct of Strawberry Hill when the Gothic Revival was to become a virulent disease.

Horace Walpole's informal Strawberry Hill Committee of Taste was to superintend the designing and building of his Gothic villa at Strawberry Hill, Twickenham. The two principals under Walpole were John Chute (1701–76), who had inherited The Vyne in Hampshire in 1754, and Richard Bentley (1708–82), son of the famous scholar Dr Richard Bentley. But in attendance was Johann Henry Muntz, to cause Walpole much huffing and puffing, and later Thomas Pitt, 1st Baron Camelford (1737–93). Few houses have been assembled by a Committee as was Strawberry, although the pedantry of assemblage was not unlike the classical exemplars gathered together by Lord Burlington at his Chiswick villa. The mode of choice was obviously conversational, sitting around a table with Walpole scrutinizing designs and making decisions. At Strawberry Walpole confessed that Chute was 'my oracle in taste, the standard to whom I submitted my trifles, and the genius that presided over poor Strawberry'. That genius is apparent on the exterior, but it was Bentley who contributed to much of the interior – the hall and staircase, the screen in the Holbein Chamber, and several chimney-pieces, between 1751 and 1761. Howard Colvin has described Bentley as a Georgian Rex Whistler, for his talents extended to book illustration, notably the 1753 Strawberry Hill Press edition of Thomas Gray's *Poems*. Whilst under Walpole's patronage and protection Bentley made designs for a Gothic 'umbrello' in the Menagerie Wood at Wentworth Castle, Yorkshire, in 1756, a Gothic Columbarium for The Vyne in 1757, St Hubert's Priory, for Henrietta, Countess of Suffolk's

Richard Bentley by John Giles Eccardt (1740–79), 1753
© National Portrait Gallery, London

Above: Donnington Grove, gallery and lantern
Henson/Country Life Picture Library

Opposite: John Chute by Gabriel Mathias (1719–1804), 1758
© National Trust Photo Library

farm at Marble Hill, Twickenham, in 1758, and a Gothic Cloister to Richard Bateman's 'half Gothick, half Attic, half Chinese and completely fribble house' at Old Windsor, Berkshire, where Muntz added the still existing octagonal Gothic room in 1761–62.

Chute had spent more than six years in Italy, and he was in Florence in 1740 when Walpole described him as 'an able Geometrician, . . . an Exquisite Architect, & of the purest taste both in the Grecian & Gothic Styles'. These encomiums are not borne out by any surviving drawings from this Italianate period, only later by a considerable corpus of brilliant sketches, not the least what he proposed for the rebuilding of Hagley and his own Vyne in Hampshire, where the staircase constructed in 1770 is a marvel of classical ingenuity. There is also album of 64 designs for the Gothic Donnington Grove, Berkshire, built for his antiquary friend James Pettit Andrews in 1763.

Bentley quarrelled with Walpole, as had Muntz, and left his employment in 1761. But Thomas Pitt, 1st Baron Camelford was on hand, when in 1762 he took the lease of a small house at Twickenham, dubbed by Walpole the 'Palazzo Pitti'. He joined Chute on the Committee, as 'one of the very few that I reckon quite worthy of being at home in Strawberry'. Pitt advised Walpole on internal decoration and designed the 'ornaments' of the Gallery and Chapel. Through Walpole's influence, in 1763 his is the Gothic Cottage, the Bridge of Rocks and a conservatory for General Conway at Park Place, Henley. But he was also a pure classicist, for in 1764 the Palladian Bridge at Hagley was his, and at Stowe, Buckinghamshire, for his near relative Richard Grenville, Lord Temple, he designed not only the Corinthian Arch in 1765, but was seemingly responsible for the final form of the south front between 1772 and 1777. Reverting to Walpolean Gothic, he designed the furnishings for the choir of Carlisle Cathedral in 1765 and alterations to the choir at Norwich in 1766. Surprisingly, Pitt was one of Sir John Soane's earliest patrons, and it was Soane who paid tribute in his *Memoirs* to his 'classical taste and profound architectural knowledge', linking his name with those of Lords Burlington and Pembroke, a hint that Pitt's classical work was regarded as more serious than his Gothic.

The Gothic Revival was greatly enriched by Sir Roger Newdigate (1719–1806), whose Arbury Hall, Warwickshire, has been described as the Strawberry Hill of the Midlands. Here could be found as builders and executants the Hiorne family of architects operating from Warwick, and some-

Arbury Hall, dining-room   Gunn/Country Life Picture Library what later Henry Keene, the builder of Newdigate's Harefield Place and alterations to the church there in 1768, as well as alterations to Newdigate's London house in Spring Gardens, 1763, and internal Gothic work at his Astley church, Warwick. Indeed, it is sometimes difficult to distinguish between the shared Gothic of these Midland patrons and architects, as occurred at University College, Oxford, where Keene remodelled the hall in Gothic in 1766, but Newdigate gave the chimney-piece to his own design. Even more confusing in this Midlands Gothic world is the intervention of Sanderson Miller (1716–80), who assisted Newdigate at Arbury in 1750–52. Although a landed gentleman of substantial means, he acted as a thorough professional with more than forty buildings to his credit between 1743 and 1780, and it is possible that like Lord Burlington he too was professionally involved in the practice of architecture.

THE AMATEUR AS INNOVATOR

The pleasure in studying these amateurs is less in trying to categorize them, than to enjoy the diversity of their architectural accomplishments. Often their work rises to distinction owing to an untrammelled attitude to design. Richard Jones, 1st Earl of Ranelagh (1638–1712), who 'spent more money, built more fine houses, and laid out more on household-furniture and gardening, than any other Nobleman in England', is known as the designer in 1688–89 of his own house adjacent to Chelsea Hospital where he was Treasurer. It was in a conservative Wrennian red brick style, not unlike a taller version of Wren's Winslow Hall, Buckinghamshire. About 1679 he had been advising Lord Conway at his houses of Ragley Hall, Warwickshire, and Newmarket, Cambridgeshire, and when appointed by William III in June 1701 as 'Sur-intendent generall of oure Buildings & of our works in our parks', which included work for himself at Cranbourn Lodge in Windsor Great Park, this appointment probably led to the additions he designed in 1704 to the Duke of Ormonde's Richmond Lodge. This too would appear to have been conventional, but before Ranelagh's death in 1712 Dr George Clarke sketched an elevation that if it does record a design by Ranelagh for converting Ranelagh House into a Thames-side Palladian villa with a Venetian Brenta style façade before 1712, is precocious, for its time far more advanced than the multitude of designs made by Ranelagh's crony Lord Mar.

In his will Ranelagh left his 'scriptore' with two drawers of mathematical instruments, rulers and perspective glasses to his 'dear friend, John Earl of Mar'. John Erskine, 11th Earl of Mar (1675–1732) might claim to be the arch Scottish amateur, for whom political intrigue and architecture were ruling passions. Mar's actual achievement on the ground in Scotland was not great, for after heading the

Above: Mezzotint of John Erskine, 6th Earl of Mar by John Smith, after Sir Godfrey Kneller (1646–1723), 1703 © National Portrait Gallery, London   *Opposite:* Triumphal Arch at Garendon Park © Crown copyright.NMR

Pretender's forces in Scotland in 1715, defeat at Sherrifmuir sent him into exile, first to Italy in 1717, Geneva and France in 1719, Paris until 1729, and finally for his health to Aix-la-Chapelle, where he died in 1732. He was a paper genius, for his was a fertile imagination prophetic of so much, borne out by the mass of his surviving architectural designs. He seems to have meddled everywhere with little consequence, at Longleat, Wilton, Bretton, Drumlanrig, Rokeby, or Wolterton. In general he delighted in offering new designs for doing up older houses, such as the house of his neighbour in Twickenham, the Hon. James Johnston, which had been designed by John James in 1710, and

extended by James Gibbs, Mar's friend, in 1720. As early as 1718 Mar was designing a house based upon the Maison Carré at Nimes, complaining that Italian architects 'will be originals and leave the example [of antiquity] and all its noble simplicity for trifling gimcrack insignificant ornaments worthy of nobody but Vanbruge'.

Not impossibly Ambrose Phillips (1707–37), and Lord Mar could have crossed continental paths, for both were fascinated by the Roman architecture of Provence. Had Phillips lived beyond the age of thirty, his name might have become a byword with those of Burlington and Pembroke, so exceptional and original was his study of antique Roman architecture, and for this he was elected a founding member of the Society of Dilettanti. On his return to England he passed through Provence to Montpellier, where he drew the Porte du Peyrou and made designs for completing the Place Royale du Peyrou in a style that must have made the French blink, for it was a study in an antique-laced, neo-Palladian English architecture, unique in France. At his estate of Garendon in Leicestershire, inherited in 1729, Phillips created a remarkable templescape with a Triumphal Arch, Temple of Venus, porticoed Summer House, and an Obelisk. His incomplete house, boasting an Ionic portico with coffering deriving from the Temple of the Sun, suggests that he had visited Bath to examine the work of John Wood the elder. There is also a link with Lord Burlington, for the courtyard entrances to Garendon are based upon Inigo Jones's unpublished Beaufort House gateway at Chiswick House.

Phillips did not design for others, and belongs to that category of the amateur who concentrates his architectural enthusiasms solely upon his own house and estate. One such, and an exceptional personality to boot, was Sir Thomas Parkyns (1662–1741), who from 1684 became squire of Bunny Hall, Nottinghamshire, as landowner, magistrate, pugilist and wrestler, described as having 'a competent knowledge of most part of the Mathematicks, especially Architecture and hydraulics, & Contriving & Drawing all his Plann̄s without an Architect'. Bunny Hall, dated 1723 with its castellated tower emerging out of a huge segmental pediment, below which is a vast escutcheon, has rightly been described as 'loony Baroque', even if it does not qualify as innovative in a progressive sense. In the same style, but more conventional, Parkyns 'Built the Schoolhouse and Hospital . . . the Mannor Houses in Bunney and East Leake [1704] . . . the Vicaridge House & most of the Farm Houses in Bunney & Bradmore.' It is not easy to categorize the style of his building, except to

Doric Gate at Garendon Park

suggest Flemish or Low Countries Baroque.

A pale comparison is John Buxton (1685–1731), a Norfolk squire, 'of some ability as an amateur architect', whose architectural scratches are hilariously tame. He scribbled away for himself, relations and friends, producing crude design after crude design constantly through the 1720s into the 1730s, for Bixley Hall, for his cousin Sir Edward Ward; for his own house at Earsham before he sold it in 1721; for his next house at Channons Hall, 1721–24; and finally for a new house at Shadwell Lodge, 1720–30. The description of him as 'a fine genius very curious in such designs', must be taken with a pinch of salt, for he was no more than competent, the look of the final building obviously due to the efficiency of the builders.

Robert Hampden Trevor (1706–83), 1st Viscount Hampden and 4th Baron Trevor, could have been allied in this account with Sir Thomas Robinson, for there are Yorkshire and Durham connections that link him to his brother Richard Trevor, Bishop of Durham, and the owner of Glynde in Sussex, where both Robinson and Robert Trevor vied to design Glynde church in 1763. Trevor's extraordinary design based on a plan of interlocking hexagons is unique outside the Baroque of Guarini or Juvarra, unless one includes the wild Baroque designs made by John Talman earlier in the century. Trevor competed for the Radcliffe Library in 1737, no doubt through his influence as

Ceiling of Gothic ruin at Fawley Court.   Photo: Robert Hradsky

a bibliophile and distinguished Latinist. His daughter Maria Constantia was engaged to be married to Francis Child of Osterley before Child's sudden death in 1763. Her father was Child's mentor in architectural matters. His surviving drawings are professionally presented and there are probably buildings by him that defy identification, such as a clever plan for a house in Spring Gardens, St James's Park, or a rotunda staircase inscribed in French 'L'idée d'un Grand Escalier for my Lord Foley', possibly for Foley's Paris hôtel. As the scion of a family landed at Hampden House Buckinghamshire, where Trevor may have built the Gothick additions, he surely knew of the amateur endeavours of Lord Camelford at Stowe, and particularly of John Freeman in the southern end of the county.

John Freeman (c.1689–1752) of Fawley Court, Bucks., confined his amateur enthusiasms to his Wrennian house of 1684 and to the laying out of its gardens beside the Thames near Henley. He created follies, many built in local Buckinghamshire knapped flint, of which the most remarkable was the Gothic Ruin combined with a Watergate and Bridge, its domed room with a flint and knuckle-bone ceiling to offset the classical antiquities, including some Arundel marbles, dug up and shared by Freeman and his friend Edmund Waller of Hall Barn, Beaconsfield, also in the county. In 1732, and probably earlier, the Gothic Ruin ranks as among the first of Gothick garden buildings in England. As a Director of the East India Company Freeman wrote to Governor John Pitt at Fort St George, Madras, that he was 'planting trees, making theatres, & building castles in the air' in the adjacent Henley Park, an estate bought in 1731. He would have received the enthusiastic imprimatur of Ambrose Phillips when be built his family Mausoleum in 1750, based upon an antique Roman design by G. B. Montano, whose book he possessed in his library.

Thomas Wright (1711–86), familiarly known as the Wizard of Durham, was the arch amateur architect of them all. In the very year that Lord Holland was building his Roman villa at Kingsgate (see p.22) so had Wright been building at Byers Green in Durham, a Roman *villula* for himself, with *suggestia* or courts, a small *praetorium* for the view of a Roman circus that he would restore in 1778, and an interior with prints illustrating the faculties of human knowledge and passions. It would have received the imprimatur of Pliny. It is surprising that Wright does not appear in the architectural genealogies of the Yorkshire Connection. Even at the age of 14 Wright was 'much in love with Mathematics' and 'very much given to the Amusements of Drawing, Planning of Maps and Buildings'.

Thomas Wright, 'Wizard of Durham'

As an astronomer he wrote many books, notably *An Original Theory or New Hypothesis of the Universe*, in 1750. He discovered the Milky Way, and spent his life passing through the orbits or genealogies of linked families, teaching astronomy, mathematics, and the polite arts, and en route designing buildings. In 1755 and 1758 he produced two volumes of *Arbours* and *Grottoes*, among the most beautiful architectural or garden design books of the age. There are curious parallels with William Kent, whom he could have met at Badminton in 1747, for like Kent he was much loved, and accepted as a member of the family. His draughtsmanship is peculiarly Kentian, and he too pioneered on paper the natural presentation of architectural designs in a landscape. A true amateur, he never appears as having been paid for his services. His was an extraordinary architectural achievement numbering more than 30 garden buildings alone between 1740 and 1780, including grottoes, root houses, eye-catchers, farms, toy forts, rocky bridges, hermitages, menageries, and many examples of early *cottages ornés*. His was the design in 1754 of Nuthall Temple, Nottinghamshire, one of the four great rotunda Palladian villas of England, and for Lord Halifax in the early 1760s he designed the new front to Horton House, Northamptonshire, the famous Menagerie there, and Hampton Court House, Middlesex, with its grotto and garden.

Antique Rome was the theme of Kingsgate on the Isle of Thanet, perhaps the most astonishing seaside villa built since Vanbrugh's Seaton Delaval in Northumberland. This cliff-top mansion near 250 feet in front was begun in 1762 for Henry Fox, 1st Lord Holland, on the model of Cicero's Formian Villa at Baiae, but more probably, Pliny's Laurentian Villa, and was designed by the eccentric Thomas Wynn, 1st Lord Newborough (1736–1807), who had studied architecture at the Turin Academy with the future Lord Grantham in 1760. A huge six-column Roman Doric portico opened to a neo-classic square entrance hall, off which were two courtyards entered from the front by triumphal arches. Initially the executant was John Vardy. Newborough was eccentric and improvident. By 1782 having spent a fortune on his own estate at Glynlliffon, Caernarvonshire, building the two expensive Forts Belan and Williamsburg, and funding the Caernarvonshire Militia, in anticipation of invasion by the French, he was forced to alleviate his fortunes in Italy, where Lady Newborough suddenly died in Leghorn, and his ten-year-old son was 'allowed to run wild'. If this was not enough, Newborough took up with Stella Chiappini, an 'Italian singing girl about 13 years old', described as 'wilder than a

Thomas Hope by Sir William Beechey (1753–1839), *c*.1799
© National Portrait Gallery, London

colt', who in rebuff described him as a 'stout old grey beard, from behind whose few and discoloured teeth came forth an offensive breath'. He married her in 1786. Back in England by 1792, Lord Holland may have employed Newborough to surround his seaside villa with a bizarre collection of follies that he had specially engraved by Basire in bistre wash. In 1805 for Holland's son, Charles James Fox, Newborough designed the Temple of Friendship at St Anne's Hill, Surrey, to display Nollekens's busts of Fox and his father.

If the French were the cause of Newborough's troubles, so were they the reason for hugely wealthy Thomas Hope (1760–1831) to exile himself from Holland to London in 1795. Hope had travelled extensively in Europe and the Near East making many architectural observations and drawings. He bought Duchess Street off Portland Place in 1799, the house built by Robert Adam for General Clerk in 1768, and in 1807 bought the Deepdene, a mid-18th-century house that Hope enlarged in two stages in 1818 and 1823. His executant architect there was the dull but efficient William Atkinson, who in no way could have contributed to the originality of Hope's Picturesque design, where in C R Cockerell's words 'the *genius loci* is so

The portico at Belsay   Henson/Country Life Picture Library

remarkably recalled'. In Duchess Street his first architect was C H Tatham, who prepared a set of designs for the Sculpture Gallery in 1809. Whether Tatham continued to be Hope's architect is uncertain, for there is some circumstantial evidence that the interests of both patron and architect were too similar for a continuing harmony. Hope's own *Household Furniture* of 1807 was much indebted to Tatham's publications. It is telling that apart from Tatham's designs, the one and only design for any other interior of Hope's houses is for his Picture Gallery, fully drawn out by Hope himself, and amply annotated by him with instructions to the executant. Hope was socially and artistically a powerful figure. His *Observations on the Plans and Elevations designed by James Wyatt, Architect for Downing College, Camb.; in a letter to Francis Annesley, Esq., M.P.*, 1804, in successfully discrediting Wyatt's Roman Doric design in favour of William Wilkins' Greek one, was proof that Hope was the 'Judge Supreme of Architecture'.

At Duchess Street and the Deepdene, Hope had needed an executant to prepare all the necessary working drawings and to organize the craftsmen. He would scrutinize, but not participate in practical building. It was quite different with Sir Charles Monck (1779–1867), who took the name of Monck on inheriting the Middleton's Caenby estates in Lincolnshire, and in 1795 inheriting from his father Sir William Middleton, old Belsay Castle in Northumberland. In 1804 he and his wife set off with the archaeologist Sir William Gell for an extensive study tour of Greece. Upon their return in 1807 Monck laid the foundations of the new Belsay Castle, Northumberland, with the intention that they perfect an adaptation of Greek architecture for domestic purposes. Monck stands alone among all amateurs in confronting and successfully realizing the whole building process, whether for the main house or secondary estate accommodation, drawing up all designs, working drawings and large scale details, and scrutinizing the very minutiae of construction. It was an astonishing achievement maturing for more than thirty years until the 1840s. In particular Monck stressed the quality and the cutting and presentation of stonework, what the French called stereotomy, which is so evident in the finished house, sitting in the centre of a romantic Picturesque garden and an ideal farming estate.

Had Wright, or indeed Holland or Freeman, been of a later generation he would surely have found empathy with Ashley Combe on its headland above Porlock Weir in Somerset, and have struck up an instant friendship there with Ada, Lady Lovelace. Her remote and favoured Somerset estate was a Plinean seaside villa, Italianate in parts, approached by a dark carriage tunnel struck 100 yards through the cliffs, debouching the visitor on to a

Augusta Ada, Countess of Lovelace by William Henry Mote, after Alfred Edward Chalon (1780–1860), 1839
© National Portrait Gallery, London

Ashley Combe in ruins *c*.1900   English Heritage.NMR

plateau with glorious sea views, to find a rambling *cottage ornée* first built in November 1799, but largely extended to her Tuscan designs between about 1835 and 1841, the background cliff, 'built up with three open terraces against the rock (one above the other) supported by a number of small arches, left with their hollow spaces at the back'. As can be seen today, the arches were intended to resemble the inside of a Roman coliseum. The Hon. Ada Augusta Byron (1815–52), the poet's only daughter, married Lord King of Ockham, who became 1st Earl of Lovelace in 1838. She was not only an amateur architect, but had been educated as a mathematician and scientist, her mentor in 1833 the computer pioneer, Charles Babbage, soon to share and improve his new ideas for a calculating engine. She is commemorated in the USA by software systems named 'Ada' in her honour.

Ada died prematurely in 1852, aged 37, only a year before that other remarkable lady architect, the 'calm, dignified and beautiful' Sara Losh (1785–1853), whose architecture is very different from Ada's, but like Freeman, Hope or Monck, her architectural pretensions were focused solely upon Wreay, her estate village south of Carlisle. Her achievement at Wreay cannot be understood without the knowledge that she and Katherine were inseparable sisters, inheriting Wreay in 1814, when the two made tours of France, Germany and Italy, notably in 1817. What was to be achieved at Wreay is so singular, that its genesis must lie in Sara's serious and intelligent continental observations of European building and decoration. Her debut at Wreay was the new schoolhouse in 1828 in a Pompeian style, but it was Katherine's tragic death in 1835 that had a traumatic effect upon Sara, determining her to build from 1841 a new village church of St Mary, a family mausoleum, and a graveyard enclosure, all in memory of her beloved sister. It would be no exaggeration to suggest that there is no church more original in England than the 'early Saxon or modified' Lombardic style of this church and its extraordinary iconographic ornamentation. Sara's lover was killed by an assegai on the North-West frontier, and the heart jumps to find an assegai struck into the wall of the chancel. Even more astonishing is the primitive mausoleum, described as 'Druidical' or 'Attic-Cyclopean', a description applying also to the savage stone slabs in the family grave enclosure. As Rosemary Hill has commented, Sara 'had all the innocent daring of the autodidact'.

Above: Doorway to St Mary, Wreay. Photo: Gavin Stamp
Left: Sarah Losh after T H Carrick (1802–75), from Henry Lonsdale, *The Worthies of Cumberland*, 1867–75

THE CATALOGUE

George III, design for a small palace, engraved by J J Kirby (Cat.22)

NOTES

This catalogue section has been compiled by John Harris and Robert Hradsky who are grateful for contributions by Dr Iain Gordon Brown on Andrew Fletcher; Gareth Williams on Lady Wilbraham and Dr Rosemary Hill on Sarah Losh. They also wish to thank Charles Hind for making available material relating to a number of the architects featured in this catalogue and exhibition.

The authors wish to pay tribute to Sir Howard Colvin's *A Biographical Dictionary of British Architects 1600–1840* in its third, 1995, edition (to be superseded this year by the 4th edition). His entries have been the mainstay of this catalogue section, and indeed compensate for long bibliographical lists.

All measurements are given in millimetres, height before width.

EARLY AMATEURS

Sir John Osborne (c.1550–1628) and the Salisbury House Porticus

1   John Osborne
    The Salisbury House Porticus, 1610
    Pen & ink (430 x 1716)
    The Marquess of Salisbury, Hatfield House

Although this catalogue and exhibition does not deal with the Elizabethan patron as contributing to architectural design, because Sir John Osborne so perfectly fulfills the criteria for an Elizabethan gentleman architect, he is represented here.

In the National Archives is a text that has long intrigued scholars. Its modern title is *Specification of a Plan by 'Mr Osborne' for making a 'Porticus' at the South End of the Earl of Salisbury's Garden, September 1610*. It opens with 'Osborne's' words: 'The purpose is to make a Porticus at the South end of my L. of Salisburyes garden in the Strand running in lengthe East and West and standing in bredth North and South', and so this description continues for more than 2,000 words, written most intelligently by one who possessed a thorough knowledge of architecture, in particular of Vitruvian theory, and construction. The writer was certainly neither a common artificer nor a more educated Simon Basil, who was surveyor to Salisbury House. The parameters when this Porticus could have been built are between 1605 and 1610, when the width of Lord Salisbury's garden corresponded to that of the 'Specification'. It might have been conceived as one of the 'Roman' loggias along the Thames as part of his plan for a neo-Augustan London built of stone rather than wood, and in anticipation of the King's visit to Salisbury House in 1608.

The 'Specification' has long tantalized historians, for no design existed to match it – until 2005 when Joseph Friedman discovered the drawing, exhibited here for the first time, in a portfolio of mainly late 18th-century development plans for the Cecil's Millbank estates. Reunited with its specification, it is now possible to claim that here is the most important architectural design of the whole Elizabethan and Jacobean age, a manifestation of pure Vitruvian classicism at a time when Inigo Jones was still adolescent in architecture.

The project based upon the drawing and the specification has been reconstructed on paper by Manolo Guerci as a two-storeyed loggia, on plan 70 feet in length by 12 feet 6 inches in width, its peristyle of sixteen by four Corinthian columns supporting an 'upper walke' for a promenade with views to both river and house. Surrounding this walk were not conventional balustrades, but 'fifty ballisters [rather like fluted pilasters] to runne in lenghte with fifty globes upon them', each surmounted by a bird with folded wings described as a 'Halcyon' bearing a twig with a leaf in its beak. The short sides of the 'walke' facing outwards were formed as pedimented superimposed porticoes, the whole cleverly worked out from Vitruvius, Serlio and Palladio, as well as Vredeman de Vries's *Architectura oder Bauung der Antiquen aus dem Vitruvius*, 1577.

The upshot of this discovery was the recognition that the 'Osborne' of the Porticus must be the designer of the Haynes Grange Room in the Victoria and Albert Museum, for that too was based

1

upon Serlio and the Corinthian order, and on its ceiling were flying birds of the 'Halycon' sort recommended for the ceiling of the Porticus. The room was installed at Haynes Grange either in 1754, or perhaps even earlier, when Haynes was a hunting park for Chicksands Priory, the seat of the Osborne family, a connection made by Mark Girouard, enabling us to conclude that the room was made up of material salvaged from the demolished Pigeon Gallery at Chicksands, which was described as having pigeons painted on the ceiling. The Osborne of the Specification is obviously the Sir John Osborne who succeeded to Chicksands in 1592. He had graduated from King's College, Cambridge, in 1573, the year of Dr John Caius's death, and maybe he had learnt something of the Doctor's interest in Renaissance architecture and its treatises.

Sir Roger Pratt (1620–85)

Sir Roger Pratt was born to a landed family from Ryston Hall in Norfolk. He matriculated at Magdalen College, Oxford in 1637 and entered Inner Temple in 1639. His father Gregory, also a lawyer, died in 1640, enabling him to set off in 1643 for a six-year tour of France, Italy, Flanders and Holland, 'to give myself some convenient education' – and what an education that was! Although Pratt matriculated in law at Padua University in January 1645, law was soon superseded by architecture. The notebooks he compiled on the Continent and after his return to England in 1649 reveal an intellectual, thoughtful and practical study of Italian, French and Dutch architecture, as well as the more familiar architecture of Inigo Jones and John Webb. Although Pratt can only be credited with four houses between Coleshill, Berkshire, begun for Sir George Pratt in 1649, but only completed in 1662, and between 1663 and 1667 the other three great houses of Kingston Lacy, Dorset, Horseheath Hall, Cambridgeshire, and Clarendon House, Piccadilly, as a group they have rightly been described as among 'the most influential buildings in the history of English domestic architecture'. As eminent in his day as Sir Christopher Wren and Hugh May, in 1668 Pratt was knighted for services to architecture. In 1664 he had inherited Ryston, where today his manuscript notebooks and library remain in treasured family possession.

2   Sir Roger Pratt
    Elevation of Kingston Lacy, 1663
    Pen, ink & coloured washes (405 x 580)
    Bankes Collection, Kingston Lacy, The National Trust

This design made by Pratt for Sir Ralph Bankes shows the principal front of Kingston Lacy in Dorset as executed. The distinctive Pratt features include prominent chimneys, balustraded roof and cupola.

3–5 Sir Roger Pratt
    Architectural notebooks
    Insc: 'Sir Roger Pratt / architects memoranda / 1657 ... Ryston Hall, Downham, Norfolk'
    Insc: 'SIR ROGER PRATT. / notes on the building of Lord Clarendon's House Aug 1664 / KINGSTON LACY / 1665' written on the cover and the words 'Ryston Hall, Downham, Norfolk'
    Insc: '1670 ... A 1671'
    Bound manuscripts
    Private Collection

6   Edward Pierce
    Letter to Sir Roger Pratt with sketch of a scroll bracket
    Insc: 'For the Worshipfull Roger Pratt Esq In ye Inner Temple ... Building of Horseheath Hall / Pierces Letter, London' and 'April 24 1665'
    Pen, ink & pencil
    Private Collection

Roger North (?1653–1734)

Roger North, the youngest son of Dudley, 4th Lord North, was educated for the law, called to the Bar in 1675, and eventually became Solicitor-General to the Duke of York. In a long life of near 80 years North, like the older John Evelyn, whom he knew well, was a virtuoso, studying optics and mathematics, science and music, and soon embracing architecture, which he regarded as his 'mechanical entertainments'. He was soon amassing an architectural library, from which books he learned the 'technicalities of building' and the 'niceties of draughtsmanship'. In 1683–84 he designed the Great Gateway from the Temple into Fleet Street, notable for its simplicity of composition. He was a friend of Wren and May. His 'Essay on Building' reveals his profound knowledge of the architecture of his time. In 1690 he bought an old house at Rougham in Norfolk which he remodelled gradually, adding a wing with a portico based upon Palladio's Villa Sagredo. For this he joins that small coterie of architects at the turn of the century who anticipate the revival of Palladian architecture.

7   Sir Roger North
    Elevation of Middle Temple Gateway, c.1683
    Pen, ink & coloured washes (435 x 360)
    Private Collection

This early design is close to the executed gateway. The final entrance had a flat central arch and round-headed doorways to the flanking shops.

8   Sir Roger North
    Elevation of Rougham Hall, c.1690
    Pen, ink & grey wash (245 x 470)
    Private Collection

3–6

THE OXFORD CIRCLE

Late 17th-century Oxford was a vortex of advanced architectural ideas, in the centre of which was the learned Henry Aldrich (1648–1710), Dean of Christ Church from 1689 and Vice-Chancellor of the university from 1692-95. As one of the 'able judges of architecture' he would become involved in all Oxford's architectural endeavours until his death, acting both directly and as a conversational *éminence grise*. His architectural library, now dispersed in the general library of his college, contained more than 50 titles, many on the Antique and Antiquity. Aldrich led a movement re-assessing Inigo Jones's Palladianism and his Peckwater Quadrangle of 1706 marked a decisive moment in the emergence of a pure classicism that would supplant the Wrennian Baroque. What matters for an understanding of early neo-Palladianism is Aldrich's role as a teacher, for he was a tutor to Sir Andrew Fountaine from 1693 to 1697 and in 1705 to Henry, Lord Herbert, later 9th Earl of Pembroke. At his death Aldrich was preparing his *Elementa Architecturae*, a Vitruvian treatise on civil and military architecture, which remained incomplete. Aldrich's architectural interests are intertwined with those of the virtuoso and man of taste, Dr George Clarke (1661-1736), who succeeded him as the leading figure in the architecture of the university. By 1710 Aldrich's reputation had spread to London and Scotland, particularly to Alexander Fletcher and Robert Gregory, seeding the new revisionist style.

Henry Aldrich (1648–1710)

Henry Aldrich became Dean of Christ Church, Oxford in 1689, and served as Vice-Chancellor of the University from 1692 to 1695. Although he advised on many Oxford buildings the only certain attribution that can be made to him is Peckwater Quadrangle at Christ Church begun in 1706. His startling design is one of the forerunners of neo-Palladian urban design, anticipating Colen Campbell's designs for Grosvenor Square, London, 1725, and John Wood's for Queen Square, Bath, 1729.

Aldrich's significant contribution was the authority he brought to bear on the study of architecture and antiquity, and his knowledge of this may well have influenced Nicholas Hawksmoor's many Oxford works.

9 Andrea Palladio (translated by Charles Fairfax)
Antichità di Roma, 1709
Printed book
Worcester College, Oxford

It was Aldrich who persuaded Charles Fairfax to undertake the Latin translation of Palladio's *Antichità di Roma*, published in 1709, where in the preface Fairfax states that Palladio was Aldrich's 'professed master in architecture'.

10 Henry Aldrich
Elementorum architecturæ pars prima de architectura civili, c.1708
Printed book
Worcester College, Oxford

Only 10 copies of the first 44 pages of *Elementa Architecturae Civilis*, a Vitruvian treatise devoted to 'Civil and Military Architecture', were printed in Aldrich's lifetime.

Henry Aldrich's groundbreaking Peckwater Quadrangle at Christ Church, Oxford

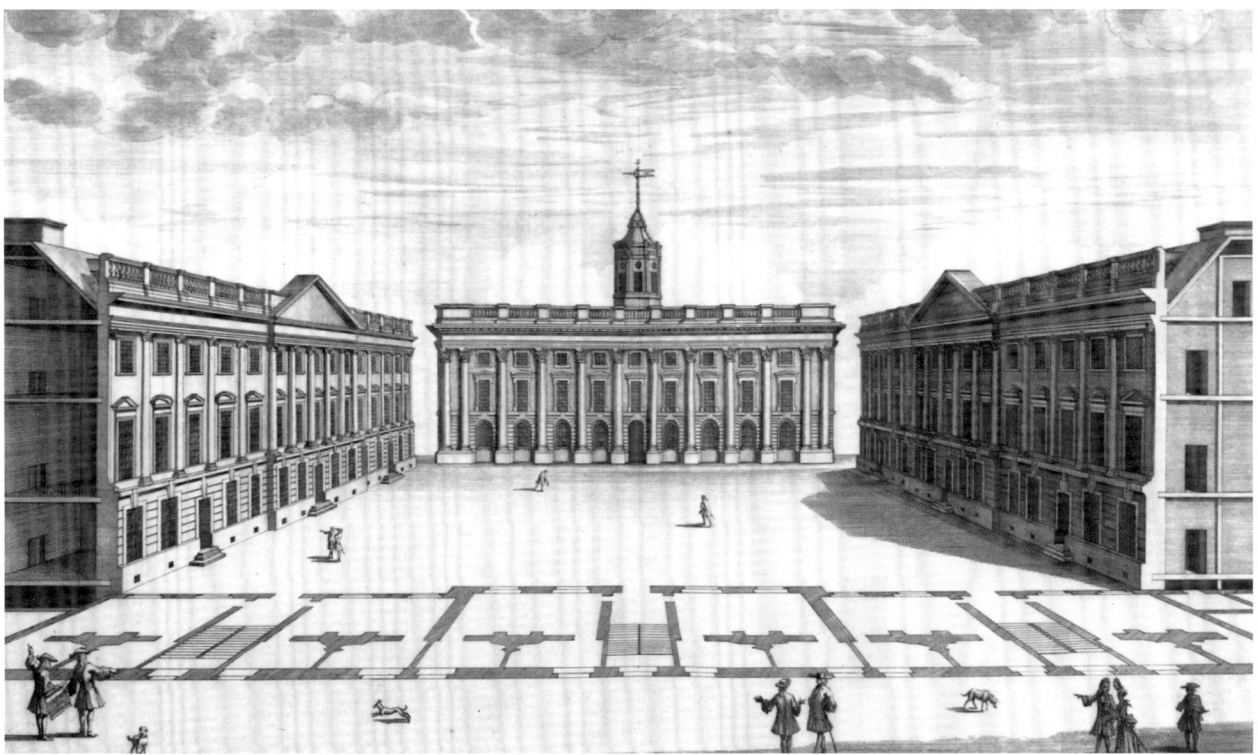

11 Henry Aldrich
Tabulae architectonicae Aldrichianae (drawings for Elementa Architecturae), *c.*1708

Bound manuscript; brown ink & grey wash with George Clarke's bookplate
Worcester College, Oxford

This bound manuscript contains the original drawings for 39 of the 55 plates in Aldrich's *Elementa Architecturae Civilis*, 1750.

12 Henry Aldrich (engraved by Sturt)
Early design for All Saints Church, Oxford, 1700

Engraving (658 x 400)
Christ Church, Oxford

13 Henry Aldrich
Teatro Olympico, Vicenza, after John Webb

Pen & ink
Worcester College, Oxford

In Aldrich's collection is the copy he made from John Webb's drawing of the Teatro Olympico in Vicenza. It seems likely that Aldrich believed that the original drawing was by Inigo Jones.

Andrew Fletcher (1653?–1716)

Andrew Fletcher of Saltoun was famous as the most combative of Scottish patriots around the time of the Union of 1707, and enjoyed a reputation as a political theorist and pamphleteer. He is also remembered as a serious book-collector and owner of perhaps the largest private library in the Scotland of his day, built up over many years of collecting in Paris and Amsterdam. Another interest was architecture, and he moved in a circle of like-minded amateurs. Fletcher is known to have designed several buildings, though in all likelihood these remained as drawing-board exercises. Through his acquaintance with the Oxford astronomer David Gregory he came to be known, at any rate by reputation, to Wren, Hawksmoor, William Talman and others of the English Baroque school.

In 1699 Fletcher designed an intriguing and enigmatic cube-shaped house. A suite of drawings survives among the Saltoun Papers in the National Library of Scotland. These show a tall, pyramidally-roofed structure, rather in the style of the contemporary Scottish proto-Palladian, James Smith. One front is three-bayed whereas the opposing front is five-bayed. It appears that these drawings accompany and illustrate - or put into words - a remarkable, long letter on architectural design as exemplified by this paper exercise in theory and style. Italian 'magnificency' is contrasted with Scottish 'meanness'. The appropriateness of differing patterns of fenestration to the Italian and Scottish climates is highlighted by Fletcher's suggestion that too many windows in a domestic building designed for Scotland made it resemble a pigeon house 'struck out all in opens'.

It seems that at some stage Fletcher's designs (if indeed the drawings really are by him) became separated from the architectural 'essay' that his letter effectively was, and another member of the family, or some other connection of the designer, attempted to construct a plan of the house based on Fletcher's verbal description, thus allowing not one but two architectural amateurs to savour the intellectual challenge of designing the cubical house.

Andrew Fletcher's design for a cube-shaped house, 1699
National Library of Scotland

Sir James Burrough (1691–1764)

Sir James Burrough acted for the University of Cambridge as Dean Aldrich and George Clarke did for Oxford. Indeed, Aldrich presented him with a copy of his *Elementa Architecturae*. He designed Stanwick Rectory, Northamptonshire, for Dr Peter Needham in 1717, the 'Manor House', Bury St Edmunds, for the Countess of Bristol in 1736, and the interior of the Norwich Assembly Rooms in 1754, but apart from these private commissions, Burrough's architectural abilities were tested in his university, in general, interior works such as the hall at Queens' College in 1732, or the remodelling of the hall and quadrangle at Trinity Hall in 1742. As early as 1721 he was associated with James Gibbs's design for the Senate House, and in 1752 he offered a design for the east front of the University Library, rejected for that executed by Stephen Wright. The Burrough's Building at Peterhouse, designed in 1736, his most publicly obvious work, is Palladian in style, but many of his designs were compromises with the work of Gibbs, whom he obviously revered.

14 Sir James Burrough
Design for Cambridge University Library, 1752

Engraving (465 x 322)
The Syndics of Cambridge University Library

30

AN OXFORD LEGACY

Sir Andrew Fountaine (1676–1753)

Sir Andrew Fountaine, of Narford Hall, Norfolk, entered Christ Church, Oxford in 1693 and graduated in 1697, his mentor there being Dean Henry Aldrich, the initiator of his interests in a Palladian Revival. It was Dean Aldrich in 1698 who selected him to give the Latin oration to William III on his entry to Oxford, for which the young man was knighted in 1699. Fountaine was the perfect virtuoso, possessing 'great Erudition'. When accompanying Thomas Herbert, 8th Earl of Pembroke, to the opening of the Irish parliament in 1707, he had probably already made the acquaintance with another of the Dean's architectural progeny, Lord Pembroke's son, Henry, the future 9th Earl. Fountaine and Lord Herbert, as he was then, were named with Lord Burlington as the three leading 'practicioners of [Palladian] architecture'. By 1717 Fountaine had laid out at Narford a remarkable garden, described by George Vertue in 1739 as 'in the best manner and wholly I believe by his own direction', that would be pivotal to the making of Burlington's own garden at Chiswick in the 1720s. From 1719–20 he added a library and courtyard range to his own design, its long elevations and the astylar façade influenced by Colen Campbell and his assistant, the young Roger Morris. Fountaine's only other documented work was a large room for the Richmond Green house of his friend Sir Matthew Decker. Although little is known about a report on 8 June 1728, in the *Norwich Gazette*, that Fountaine was 'to direct, as 'tis said, the building of a Palace at Richmond' for George II, this was the palace for which Sir Edward Lovett Pearce made designs. Fountaine's architectural library inventoried in 1731, and in 1753 following his death, was one of the most extensive of its time, containing nearly all the major Italian, French and English treatises and design books.

15 J A Dassier
Medallion of Sir Andrew Fountaine, 1744
Bronze (diam. 50)
Private Collection

Henry Herbert (c.1689–1750)

Henry Herbert, who succeeded as 9th Earl of Pembroke in 1733, matriculated in 1705 at Christ Church, Oxford, where he contributed £20 to the building of Aldrich's Peckwater Quadrangle. As an architectural progeny of Aldrich, he shares this with his great friend Sir Andrew Fountaine. Herbert's Grand Tour extended from 1711 to 1713, when he is known to have met William Kent and Lord Shaftesbury. Although he was a collector and antiquarian, architecture was his lifelong passion. Walpole regarded him as a purer architect than either Burlington or Kent, but it is probably true that Herbert did not sully himself with the building process. After Aldrich, he came first under Colen Campbell's influence and then may have met Roger Morris, Campbell's protégé. Pembroke House, Whitehall, 1724, Marble Hill, Twickenham,1724, White Lodge, Richmond,1727, Westcombe House, Blackheath, 1727, were all built by Morris, and so close is the relationship between the Architect Earl and Morris, that it is difficult to apportion responsibility, especially for what is known as Morris's cubist style of villa composition, as at Herbert's own Westcombe Lodge. The Palladian Bridge at his beloved Wilton,

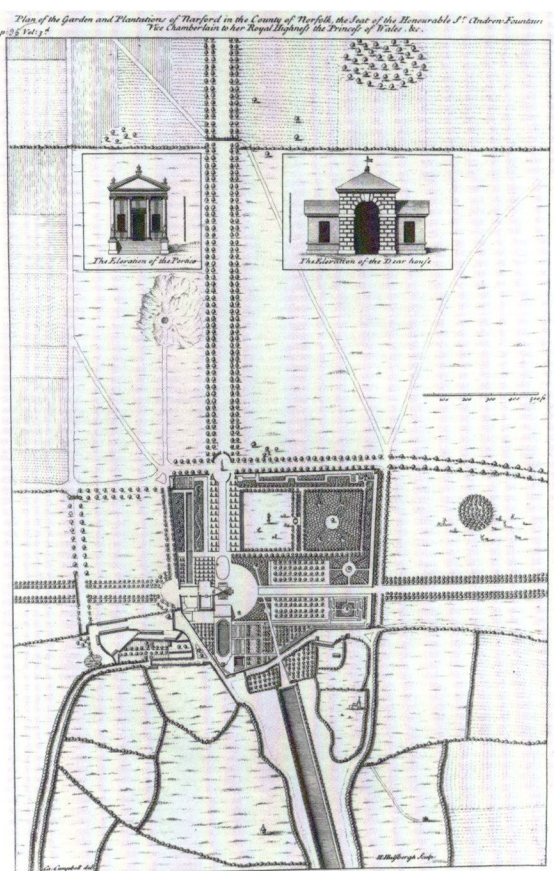

Sir Andrew Fountaine's remarkable garden at Narford, from *Vitruvius Britannicus* Vol.III

of which Vertue wrote in 1740, 'this is the design of the present Earl of Pembroke and built by his direction', is regarded as one of the most beautiful of all garden buildings. Soon after building Wimbledon House, Surrey, for Sarah, Duchess of Marlborough, in 1732, Pembroke gave Morris a silver cup, on which was engraved a portrait of Inigo Jones, and the later inscription, 'Given by my Noble Patron Henry, Earl of Pembroke, by whose favour alone I am Enabled to fill it. R. Morris 1734.'

The water house at Houghton Hall, designed by Henry Herbert
Country Life Picture Library

THE YORKSHIRE CONNECTION

Rokeby Park is at the centre of a web of Yorkshire landed amateurs, many linked by family relationships. Sir Thomas Robinson of Rokeby knew Lord Burlington well at both Chiswick and Londesborough Hall, Burlington's Yorkshire seat. Colonel James Moyser, who designed Bretton Hall, Yorkshire, in about 1730, was Burlington's disciple, and must also have been closely involved with Colen Campbell before that architect's death in 1729. Indeed, it is probable that when Moyser designed the exterior of Nostell Priory by 1731, his design was based upon one made by Campbell. Robinson of Rokeby also knew Thomas Worsley of Hovingham, and Worsley's sister had married Sir Thomas Robinson of Newby, who succeeded as 2nd Baron Grantham in 1770. Robinson's son, Thomas Philip, Earl de Grey, was the architect of his own Wrest Park, Bedfordshire, and became the first President of the Institute of British Architects.

Richard Boyle, 3rd Earl of Burlington (1694–1753)

Richard Boyle, 3rd Earl of Burlington, dedicated himself as no other nobleman to architecture, so much so that on 17 October 1749, Lord Chesterfield could write to his son, 'You may soon be acquainted with the considerable parts of civil architecture; and for the minute and mechanical parts of it, leave them to masons, bricklayers and Lord Burlington, who has to a certain degree, lessened himself by knowing them too well.' Before Burlington had committed himself to architecture he had employed James Gibbs and Colen Campbell, the latter describing the Bagnio at Chiswick as 'the first essay of his Lordship's happy invention, 1717'. This early Burlington could be described as an amateur. However, the decisive transitional year is 1719 when he returned from Italy with William Kent and took personal control at both Burlington House and Chiswick. By 1720 his drawing office had been set up in the Bagnio, guarded at its entrance by the statues of Palladio and Jones, and Henry Flitcroft was employed as a draughtsman and Clerk of Works. From then on Burlington is surely acting as a professional, albeit a gentleman, architect, who would eventually involve himself in the building of more than 30 projects. Many of his early designs demonstrate his method: to draw out immaturely a sketched or washed design in plan and elevation and to pass it on to Flitcroft for precise re-drawing, sometimes with the instructions, 'Draw this out by tomorrow morning' or words to that effect. Although denying Burlington the status of an amateur, it must be recognized that he stood at the centre of a web of amateur endeavour that embraced Sir Andrew Fountaine, Henry, Lord Herbert, Sir Thomas Robinson and Colonel Moyser.

Thomas Worsley (1711–78)

Thomas Worsley of Hovingham Hall, Yorkshire, succeeded his father in 1750. It was then that he contemplated a new house built to his own designs, a building that would progress in fits and starts for nearly twenty years. Two documents reveal his early interest in architecture, a drawing of a Doric order inscribed 'T W Etonensis 1728', and the learning manual, William Salmon's *Art of Drawing*, 1701, inscribed 'T Worsley 1722 Ex Libris T Worsley Etonensis 1726'. On his Grand Tour from 1735–38 Worsley was in Florence, Rome, Geneva, and lastly in Paris.

A clue to the origins of his architectural enthusiasms must lie with his mother, who was the sister of Sir Thomas Frankland of nearby Thirkelby Park. At Frankland's death in 1747 his library, sold by Samuel Baker on 18 and 19 June that year, is revealed as the finest architectural library in the north of England. Suggestively, Sir Thomas may have been Worsley's mentor. Horace Walpole described Worsley as 'a creature of Lord Bute, and a kind of riding-

16

master to the King'. Houses and architecture were Worsley's twin passions and, as early as 1743, he was advising Bute on building the riding house at Mount Stuart, and a year later had designed stables at Marske Hall near Richmond for John Hutton.

In 1760 Bute undoubtedly recommended Worsley to George III to be Surveyor-General of the King's Works, then a political appointment, when Henry Flitcroft was Comptroller and William Chambers and Robert Adam the newly appointed Joint Architects to the King. Worsley was an attentive Surveyor, advising on Chambers's design for the Riding House at Buckingham House. In fact, he and Chambers remained the closest of friends until Worsley's death. As an architectural enthusiast Worsley borrowed or purloined many 'office' designs for his own collection using them as exemplars.

Worsley's surviving 28 drawings for the house illustrate his progressive thinking, first simply for a courtyard stable block, then for a pedimented centrepiece to the main wing of the stables, then to the momentous decision to combine stables, riding house and the Hunting Hall with the domestic apartments as one entity – Hovingham as it is today. The inspiration was Palladio's reconstruction of a Roman House from book four of his *Quattro Libri*, Worsley having bought the first 1570 edition in 1757. Memorable are Chambers's recollections of the screams of pain to be heard throughout the house from Worsley's suffering from the stone, from which he died.

16–18 Thomas Worsley
Designs for Hovingham Hall
Pencil, pen & coloured washes (441 x 405; 360 x 510; 330 x 549)
Worsley Collection

19 & 20 Thomas Worsley
Designs for a domed temple
Pen & coloured washes (257 x 382; 300 x 169)
Worsley Collection

21 Thomas Worsley
Drawing for Doric Order
Pen & ink (376 x 303)
Worsley Collection

George III (1738–1820)

There is more surviving paper evidence of architectural design for George III than for any other European monarch. When his father, Frederick, Prince of Wales, died suddenly in 1751 Kew Gardens was in the throes of new works that had been in progress since 1748. There is evidence that in the summer of 1749 William Chambers had been consulted by Prince Frederick and the Princess Augusta as an expert, having just returned from China. In 1756 Chambers was appointed architectural tutor to George, Prince of Wales. No prince could have been better served, for in 1757 the Dowager Princess Augusta commanded Chambers to design and lay out new gardens, and over the next two years Chambers used his tuition to compose his masterful *Treatise on Civil Architecture*, 1759. Not only did Prince George learn paper design, but it was a learning based upon the practical building of more than seventeen temples and garden ornaments. For the next thirty years George III took a continued interest in the royal works, notably the remodelling of Buckingham House, and in the many projects for a new palace at Richmond. Indeed, it is likely that the model for Richmond Palace in 1762 was a joint effort of the king and Chambers.

22 George III
Plate from John Joshua Kirby, The Perspective of Architecture … deduced from the Principles of Dr. Brook Taylor, 1761, from a design by George III for a small palace

Engraving (380 x 564)
Worsley Collection

23 George III
Design for a doorway at Buckingham House

Pen & coloured washes (252 x 153)
Worsley Collection

24 Lucius Gahagan (attrib.) (1773–1855)
Statuette of George III, c.1800

Bronze (h. 150)
Private Collection

Sir Thomas Robinson (c. 1702–77)

Sir Thomas Robinson, the heir of Rokeby, Yorkshire, commissioned a design for a new house in 1724 from the York architect William Wakefield. This he rejected by 1725, and decided to design his own house, based upon Pliny's villa at Tusculum. In 1728 he married the eldest daughter of Charles Howard, 3rd Earl of Carlisle, and they set out together for continental travels, returning in 1731. Between 1735 and 1741 Robinson issued a set of engraved designs for Rokeby signed 'T. Robinson Bar. Architectus', probably drawn by Isaac Ware, who may have been his amanuensis. The house was long in building, for Robinson's was an expensive lifestyle, resulting in his departure for Barbados in 1741 as Governor in order to relieve his finances. He designed many buildings there. He returned to London in 1747 and, in 1749, built himself a house in Whitehall. Also, in his capacity as Master of Ceremonies at Ranelagh Gardens he built a large Prospect Place adjacent to the Gardens. His correspondence with his father-in-law Lord Carlisle on architectural matters reveals his deep, sensitive, and thoroughly professional knowledge of architecture. His was the distinguished Kentian-style western court at Castle Howard built between 1753 and 1759. For Ralph, 2nd Lord Verney, one of the proprietors of Ranelagh Gardens, at Claydon House, Buckinghamshire, he began to build a huge new range containing magnificent state rooms, incomplete at Robinson's death in 1777. They would have bankrupted his lordship.

25 Sir Thomas Robinson
Bird's-eye view of Rokeby Hall (north elevation), c.1740

Engraving (312 x 470)
The Dean and Chapter of York

26 Sir Thomas Robinson
Design for the west front of Claydon House, Buckinghamshire, c.1777

Pen, ink & grey wash (829 x 1219)
Claydon House Trust

Thomas Robinson, 2nd Baron Grantham (1738–86)

Thomas Robinson succeeded Sir Thomas Robinson of Newby Hall, Yorks, as 2nd Baron Grantham. His interest in architecture may have been encouraged by Thomas Worsley of Hovingham, his uncle on his mother's side. As far as we know he was a paper architect, although one of real ability, possessing an attractive draughting style. He was celebrated in Italy 1759-61 as a most knowing connoisseur, where he is found studying at the Academy in Turin with Lord Newborough in 1759. Upon his return he was elected to the Society of Dilettanti and the Society of Antiquaries in 1763. Among his designs was a Triumphal Arch at Hyde Park Corner in 1761, offices, stables and garden buildings at Newby Park, the Colen Campbell house, now known as Baldersby, and a prospect tower for his brother-in-law John Parker of Saltram. As Ambassador in Madrid from 1771 to 1779, his correspondence with Sir William Chambers underlines his very competent knowledge of architecture.

27 Thomas Robinson
Elevation of triumphal arch for Hyde Park Corner, 1761

Pen & ink (380 x 580)
West Yorkshire Archives

28 Thomas Robinson
Elevation of a tower, Saltram, c.1769

Pencil, pen & brown wash (800 x 590)
West Yorkshire Archives

29 Thomas Robinson
The Root House, Newby Park, 1785

Pen, ink & coloured washes (560 x 740)
West Yorkshire Archives

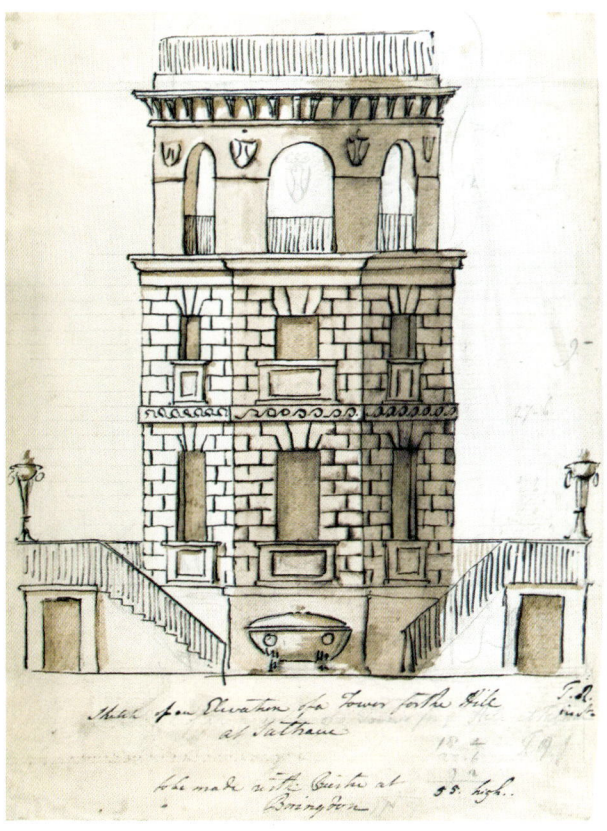

Colonel James Moyser (c.1688–1751)

Colonel James Moyser of Beverley was an officer in the regiment of foot of Sir Charles Hotham, who had employed Campbell to design his house in Eastgate of that town in 1716. In Spain Colonel Moyser was Adjutant to the 1st Earl Stanhope, and so might have been expected to have been aware of the 'New Junta for Architecture', a Palladian movement supported by Stanhope in contention with the Baroque of Vanbrugh. Exactly how Moyser became interested in architecture is unclear. He was certainly a friend of Lord Burlington. He assisted Sir William Wentworth in the design of Bretton Hall, Yorkshire, c.1730, and in 1746 offered designs for Gunthwaite, as 'the most convenient, the handsomest, and the cheapest of any House in Yorkshire', and to Stephen Thompson for Kirby Hall, also Yorkshire, its plan 'a perfect Model of Ld. Orford's at Houghton'. However, it is for the elevations of Nostell Priory that Moyser's skill as an amateur architect must be judged. There is little originality and a certain dullness in the proportions. Campbell almost certainly offered designs before his death in 1729, and these designs, based on a plan of Palladio's Villa Mocenigo, relating also to Houghton, were passed on to Moyser by 1731. However the house was not begun until 1737.

Nostell Priory

Thomas Philip De Grey, Earl de Grey (1781–1859)

Thomas Philip De Grey, Earl de Grey, was born the elder son of Thomas Robinson, 2nd Baron Grantham, from whom he might have inherited amateur architectural interests, but only as genes, for his father died in 1786 when Thomas Philip aged five became 3rd Baron Grantham. His mother was Mary, second daughter of Philip Yorke, 2nd Earl of Hardwick, and Jemima, Marchioness Grey of Wrest Park. Thomas Philip's family seat was Newby Park (renamed Baldersby), a Colen Campbell villa. Under the will of William Weddell, a distant relative, he inherited Newby Hall, so confusingly becoming the owner of two seats of the same name. At the Campbell Newby he added a dining-room to his own design in 1808, the executant architect being John Shaw. When he inherited Wrest Park, Bedfordshire, through his mother, he replaced the vast old house set in formal gardens with a French chateau, building between 1834 and 1839. As he wrote, 'I was strictly and in every sense of the word my own architect . . . I had my French books always under my hand'. The executant was James Clephan. Most of de Grey's designs are signed with a G surmounted with a coronet. As Howard Colvin writes, 'The result was a *tour de force* of French eighteenth-century architectural design on English soil.' Around Wrest Park his were the Silsoe Lodges and Silsoe Church, the latter in 1830–31 in an authentic Perpendicular Gothic. As one who preferred 'to move among men of letters and artists at the various learned societies of which he was a member', it was not surprising that in 1835 he was invited to be the first President of the newly founded Institute of British Architects, which position he held until his death.

30 Earl de Grey
Plan and elevation for Wrest Park, Bedfordshire c.1834

Pen, ink & coloured washes (380 x 580)
RIBA Drawings Collection

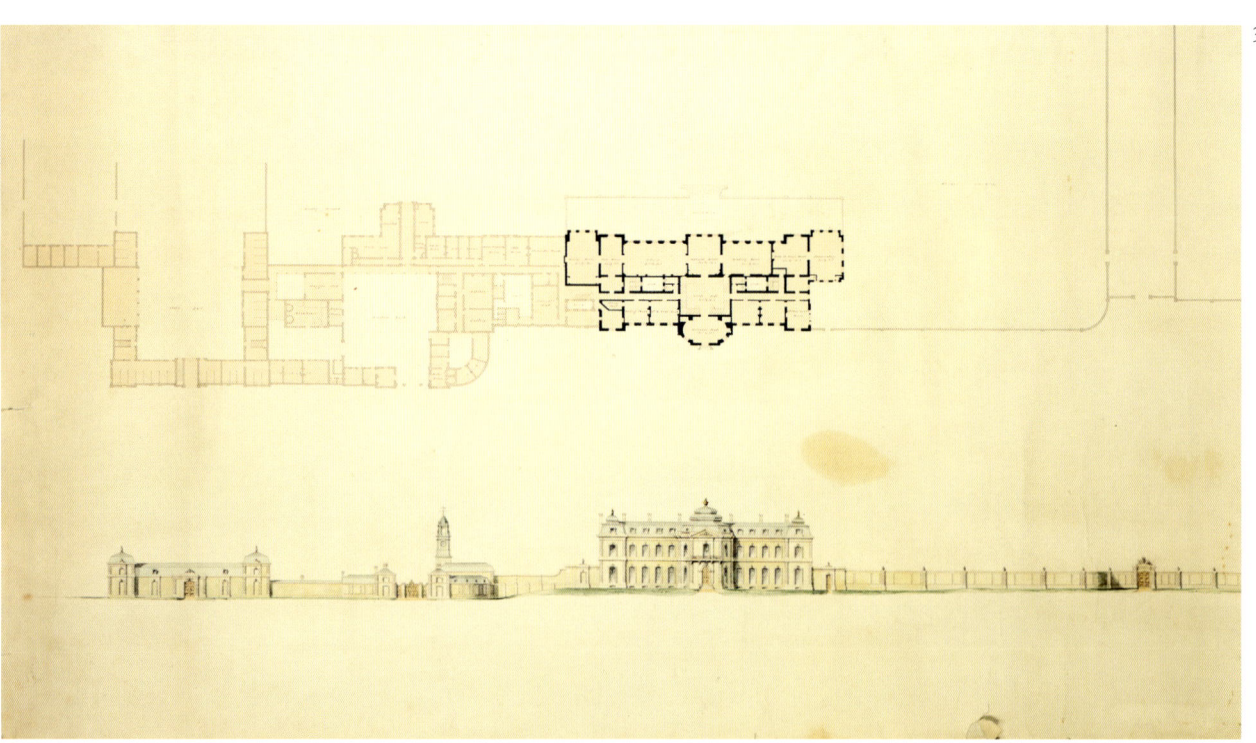

30

AMATEUR ARCHITECTS & PROFESSIONAL EXECUTANTS

Robert Dingley (1710–81)

Robert Dingley, a merchant, member of the Russia Company, Director of the Bank of England, governor of the Foundling Hospital and one of the founders of the Magdalen Hospital for penitent prostitutes, used his great wealth not only as a philanthropist, but as a collector and antiquarian, and was one of the original members of the Society of Dilettanti. His unexecuted engraved designs for the Magdalen Hospital c.1763 and for the King's and Queen's Baths in Bath, c.1766 are in a conservative Palladian style. No drawings by Dingley for them have so far been identified. It is reasonable to suggest links and friendship with Theodore Jacobsen, the Hanseatic merchant and architect of the Foundling Hospital.

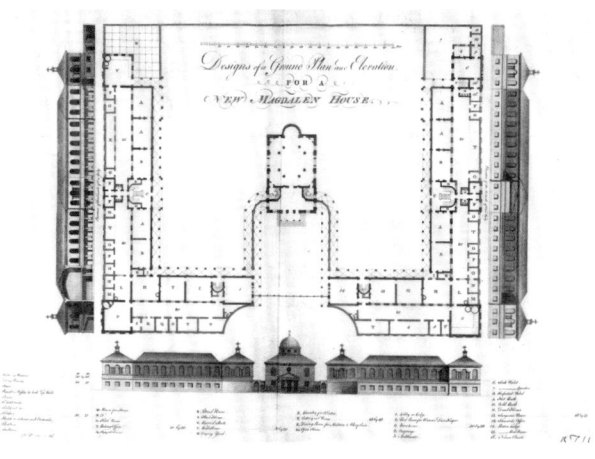

Robert Dingley's unexecuted design for Magdalen Hospital c.1763

Theodore Jacobsen (died 1772)

From 1735 Theodore Jacobsen actively managed the London Steelyard for the Hanseatic merchants. Yet he was also an amateur architect, first in 1726 for the East India Company, who adopted the 'ground plat and front presented by Theeodore Jacobsen' for their new building in Leadenhall Street. The executant was John James. There is then an unexplained hiatus, although his design for the Bank of England offered in 1731 was rejected, although engraved. His next commission was the Foundling Hospital in 1742, this time the execution entrusted to James Horne, who was also the builder from 1745 of Jacobsen's Royal Naval Hospital for Sick Sailors at Haslar near Portsmouth. In 1752 he supplied designs for Trinity College, Dublin, with Henry Keene and John Sanderson on call as builders. In general Jacobsen adopted a simple astylar elevational treatment with pavilions around a courtyard. In his will he refers to his books of architecture and a portfolio containing his designs, one of which may have been for his own house at Lonesome Lodge at Wooton in Surrey, built in 1740 for summer use.

31 Theodore Jacobsen
A View of the Foundling Hospital engraved by B Cole
Engraving (215 x 336)
Private Collection

Thomas Prowse (c.1708–67)

Thomas Prowse, representing Somerset in Parliament from 1740 until his death, was perhaps the beau idéal of the country gentleman acting as an amateur architect. Although no drawings survive by him, he was clearly a very able designer. He was friendly with two 'Sandersons', Sanderson Miller whom he advised on the design of Hagley Hall, Worcestershire, 1754–60, and John Sanderson, who was the executant of his designs, and was also involved at Hagley. Wicken church, Northamptonshire, on the estate inherited through his wife, was 'designed and built by Thomas Prowse Esqr' from 1753 in a Sanderson Miller Gothic style, assisted by John Sanderson, who also enlarged Wicken House for Prowse in 1765. Hatch Court, Somerset, was an ingenious Palladian tower villa, built for John Collins in 1755, and towers too were added to Kimberley Hall, Norfolk, under Sanderson's directions in 1755–57. The Lawn, Swindon, was refronted for Thomas Goddard in 1757; and Prowse designed the Temple of Harmony at Halswell, Somerset, built in 1764.

THE GOTHICISTS

The early Gothic Revival – often facetiously described as 'Gothic with a k', was very much the preserve of the amateur interventionists. John Freeman's Gothic Temple at Fawley is remarkably innovative, having been built before 1732. By the mid-1730s Dickie Bateman at Old Windsor had already extended his house in Gothick, and by the mid-1740s Sanderson Miller was building Gothic towers or castles around his house at Radway in Warwickshire that evoked in the mind romantic visions of knightly ancestry, or as Walpole commented, 'the true rust of the Barons' wars'. By 1750 Miller was advising Sir Roger Newdigate on Gothic work at Arbury Hall, Warwickshire, and Newdigate himself was making sketches for Gothic additions to his seat in the south at Harefield Place and church in Middlesex. Through many connections both of family and friendship there spread throughout the Midlands a web of Gothic endeavour, taken up by professionals (Henry Keene or William and John Hiorne) and amateurs alike. In fact, Miller did far more than any other amateur to spread the Gothick disease, for more than twenty of his works are in the Gothic style. Indeed Arbury served as a vortex of Midland's Gothic enthusiasm, as did Strawberry Hill in the south, where the amateur members of Horace Walpole's Committee of Taste comprised Richard Bentley between 1751 and 1761, John Chute through the 1750s, and Thomas Pitt, Lord Camelford in the 1760s. Chute, who was a professional and clever draughtsman, helped to design Chalfont House, Buckinghamshire c.1755, where Bentley designed the Gothic stables c.1760, and in 1763 designed Donnington Grove, Berkshire, for his friend the antiquary James Pettit Andrews.

John Chute (1701–76)

John Chute inherited the family seat of The Vyne in 1754. He had spent six years in Italy from 1740–46, something more than just a traditional Grand Tour, for Chute asked Horace Walpole, 'Tell me what you think of my living forever in Florence?' He studied architecture, and because Walpole thought him 'an able Geometrician, and . . . an Exquisite Architect, and of the purest taste both in the Grecian and Gothic Styles', it is not surprising that Chute soon found himself appointed to Walpole's Committee of Taste for the building of Strawberry Hill, acquired in 1747, but not begun until 1749. It would seem that initially he and Richard Bentley worked as a duo assisted by William Robinson for practical building. Only later in 1762 did Thomas Pitt join the Committee. Chute seems to have designed the elevations for the house and many of the interiors including the Gallery; he was also author, with Pitt, of much of the Gothic Chapel built in 1772. Chalfont House, Bucks. is Chute's around 1755 in Strawberry's Gothic style, so is his most successful house, Donnington Grove, Berkshire, in 1763. His drawings are a wonder, especially the many complex studies for the staircase in The Vyne, described as 'a theatrical *tour de force* that has no parallel in English country house architecture'. When Chute died in 1776 Walpole bemoaned that 'he was my oracle in taste, the standard to whom I submitted my trifles, and the genius that presided over poor Strawberry!'

32 **John Chute**
   Elevation for Strawberry Hill, 1753
   Pencil (288 x 406)
   Hampshire Record Office

33 **John Chute**
   Perspective for south front of the Vyne and other sketches,
   c.1770
   Pen & pencil (185 x 230)
   Hampshire Record Office

34 **John Chute**
   Perspective of a two-storey portico, c.1770
   Pencil (230 x 185)
   Hampshire Record Office

Staircase at The Vyne — English Heritage.NMR

Donnington Grove © Crown copyright.NMR

35

35 John Chute
Sketches in perspective of staircases, c.1770
Pen & ink (230 × 185)
Hampshire Record Office

Thomas Pitt (1737–93)

Thomas Pitt was created 1st Baron Camelford in 1784. He travelled to Spain and Portugal with Lord Strathmore in 1760, when he already made intelligent observations on Moorish and Gothic architecture. When in Florence he heard of his father's death and his succession to Boconnoc in Cornwall. In 1762 he rented a small house at Twickenham, facetiously dubbed Palazzo Pitti by Walpole, who reckoned him 'one of the very few . . . quite worthy of being at home at Strawberry'. He advised on much interior decoration there, notably the 'ornaments' of the Gallery and Chapel. How he acted as an amateur architect is uncertain, as no designs survive from his hand. His was the Gothic Cottage and Bridge of Rocks at General Conway's Park Place, Henley-on-Thames, in 1763 and the Palladian Bridge at Hagley for his uncle Sir Richard Lyttelton 'built after young Mr. Pitt's design' in 1764. The following year he designed the Corinthian Arch at Stowe House, Bucks., and it is reliably certain that he was responsible for the final form of the great south front at Stowe between 1772 and 1777. At his beloved Boconnoc, his was the south wing in a Palladian style, and Palladian also was Camelford House, Park Lane, built in 1771. He was elected to the Society of Dilettanti in 1763, and in 1785 was unsuccessful in persuading the Society to convert two of his houses in Hereford Street into a museum. Surprisingly he was one of Sir John Soane's earliest patrons, and it was Soane who paid tribute in his *Memoirs* to Pitt's 'classical taste and profound architectural knowledge', and in one of his lectures coupled his name with those of Burlington and Pembroke as leaders of architectural taste in England.

The Bridge of Rocks at Park Place, designed by Thomas Pitt, 1763. Photo: Robert Hradsky

Sir Roger Newdigate (1719–1806)

Sir Roger Newdigate was a connoisseur and antiquarian. He developed his deep interest in art, architecture, and especially painting galleries on his two Italian tours in 1739–40 and 1774–75. In the latter years he was a friend and patron of Piranesi, from whom he bought 12 bound volumes of his prints, as well as a duplicate set, which he presented to the Ashmolean Museum with two of Piranesi's composed candelabra. His enthusiasms made his Arbury Hall, Warwickshire, into the Strawberry Hill of the Midlands, and as such enormously influential. Although he made many designs for it, as well as for Harefield church, and Harefield Place, Middlesex, to achieve his aims he employed a team of executants that included Sanderson Miller, the Hiornes, Henry Keene and Henry Couchman. Apart from Arbury and Harefield, the only other project he was involved in was an unexecuted Palladian design for his brother-in-law John Conyers at Copt Hall in Essex in the 1740s, a house eventually built in 1753 by John Sanderson. He endowed the Newdigate Prize for Poetry at the University of Oxford.

36 Sir Roger Newdigate
Sketches for Gothic architecture, including fan-vaulting, c.1750
Pencil (200 × 310)
Warwickshire County Record Office (by kind permission of Lord Daventry)

36

Sanderson Miller (1716–80)

Sanderson Miller in 1717 found himself the master of Radway Grange, Warwickshire, with an ample fortune to devote himself to a life of landscape gardening and architecture. His thatched cottage built at Edgehill in 1744 was one of the first, preceding even those by Thomas Wright. More than 40 works can be associated with him, and this extraordinary output between 1743 and 1766 really makes Miller a professional amateur. A great number, especially the Gothic ones, are likely to have been executed by the Hiorns of Warwick. He was an extensive correspondent, but it is still unclear how he could command such a large practice, much larger than most professionals, without a business office.

37 Sanderson Miller
Design for a room at Arbury Hall, 1750

Pencil (211 x 296)
Warwickshire County Record Office (by kind permission of Lord Daventry)

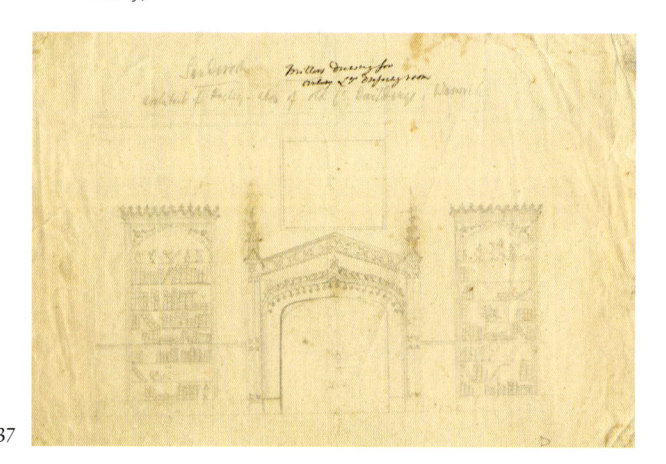

William Stukeley (1687–1765)

William Stukeley was a founder member in 1717 of what became the Society of Antiquaries. He was voted Secretary and John Talman Director. The latter was described by Stukeley as 'a gentleman who traveling into Italy, made himself a master in architecture. He drew well; had a vast collection of drawings, chiefly in ecclesiastical matters.' Both were antiquaries, who in their various ways encouraged a Gothic Revival, quite different from the Rococo Gothic of William Kent in 1732. Indeed, Talman's design for the Hall and Chapel at All Souls, Oxford, offered in March 1708, and self-confessedly, 'unlike any other in Oxon & pretty much after ye Italian Gothic' can only be compared to the 16th-century designs for the façade of S. Petronio in Bologna. However, despite an abundance of Baroque and classical designs, it is difficult to judge Talman as a gentleman amateur, for he emerged out of the professionalism and tuition of his father William.

Stukeley is different. As a founder member of the Egyptian Society in December 1741, a month later he introduced his friend and patron John, 2nd Duke of Montagu (1690–1749), who can also claim to be an amateur architect, with, in Stukeley's words 'a very good knack of drawing and designing'. Montagu had a hand in the designs for Clitheroe Castle, Lancs. in 1740, the barracks at Woolwich in 1741 and many castle projects on his Northamptonshire estates. In his obituary of the Duke Stukeley wrote, 'We had exactly the same taste for old family concerns, genealogy, pictures, furniture, coats of arms, the old way of building, gardening and the like; in a general imitation of pure nature in the Gothic architecture, in painted glass, in the open hearted, candid way in designing and free manner of conversation.' In 1744 the Duke asked Stukeley for a drawing and a wooden model of a Gothic Bridge for the park at Boughton, and on 4 October 1748, 'A design for the chapel at Boughton house in the north east wing', a most precocious, daringly Gothic, fan-vaulted design that has no precedent in the Gothic Revival in England.

Above: Model of Stukeley's Gothic Bridge at Boughton
Photo by kind permission of His Grace the Duke of Buccleuch and Queensberry, KT

Left: The octagonal chamber at Warwick Shire Hall, by Sanderson Miller

THE AMATEUR AS INNOVATOR

Richard Jones, 3rd Viscount and 1st Earl of Ranelagh (?1638–1712)

Richard Jones, 3rd Viscount and 1st Earl of Ranelagh, an Irish peer, is an amateur architect for there is no surviving evidence of draughting ability. As Chancellor of the Irish Exchequer, and a friend of the Duke of Ormonde, he amassed a huge fortune from public office, and 'spent more money, built more fine houses, and laid out more on household-furniture and gardening, than any other Nobleman in England'. He advised Lord Conway in his buildings in Newmarket, Cambridgeshire, and at Ragley, Worcestershire, c.1679–80. To serve himself as Treasurer of Chelsea Hospital he built adjoining a large tall red brick house c.1688–89, not unlike a taller version of Wren's Winslow Hall, Buckinghamshire, with gardens later to become the famous Ranelagh Pleasure Gardens. In June 1700 William III made him 'Sur-intendent generall of oure Buildings & of our works in our parks', and to this end he bought from Lord Lexington Cranbourn Lodge in Windsor Great Park, extending it as well as laying out new gardens by London and Wise. In 1704 he supervised the enlargement of the Duke of Ormonde's house in Richmond Park. When he died his legacies included his two drawers of mathematical instruments, rulers and perspective glasses to his 'dear friend John, Earl of Mar', and £20 each to John Churchill, Master Carpenter and Henry Wise, Master Gardener, 'to buy silver in remembrance of me who was heartily his friend'.

38 Dr George Clarke (1661–1736)

Design for converting Ranelagh House into a Palladian Thames-side villa, c.1688

Insc: 'Ld Ranelagh's'
Pen & ink (100 x 190)
Worcester College, Oxford

This elevation of a neo-Palladian villa is a project for converting the Wren-style brick house by Chelsea Hospital, designed by the 1st Earl of Ranelagh in the 1680s, into a Palladian villa by the Thames. This precocious design by the Oxford amateur George Clarke must have been made in consultation before Ranelagh's death in 1712.

John Erskine, 6th Earl of Mar and 11th Lord Erskine (1675–1732)

Two passions dominated the life of John Erskine, 6th Earl of Mar and 11th Lord Erskine: 'political intrigue and architectural design'. For the former he suffered exile as a Jacobite, and even when he severed his connections with the Pretender's court in 1725, he was never forgiven by the English government, and died abroad in 1732. He was a paper architect, a dreamer, of whom it was said that 'his only amusement during his exile was to draw plans and designs'. No architect was more fertile in his inventions, and in the matter of the amateur intervention he was corresponding with other amateurs such as Sir Thomas Robinson at Rokeby or Sir William Wentworth and Colonel Moyser at Bretton. His is a conservative Franco-Italian influence in design, and the relationship to James Gibbs is yet to be fully investigated, as is the actual connections between Mar and the very many landowners for whom he made designs. Howard Colvin writes of him as 'a unique figure in British architectural history. Though a nostalgic fantasy runs through so many of his designs, no one can examine them without recognizing an able and fertile imagination, or fail to conclude that if Scotland had lost a lord of dubious political integrity in 1715, she also lost an amateur architect of some distinction.' Mar lived at Twickenham next door to the house of the Hon. James Johnston, Secretary for Scotland, that had been completed by John James in 1710, to which Gibbs added the Octagon Room in 1720. Mar's design 'for ornamenting Mr Johnston's house' is dated June 1721.

39 Earl of Mar

Elevation of Johnston's house Twickenham, 1721

Pen & ink (277 x 306)
National Archives of Scotland

40 Earl of Mar

Design for House of Dun, 1723

Pen, ink & coloured washes (390 x 253)
National Archives of Scotland

Ambrose Phillips (1707–37)

Ambrose Phillips was of Garendon Park, Leicestershire, an estate acquired by his grandfather in 1683. He died tragically young at the age of 30, his passion for architecture commemorated by the inscription on his tomb in Shepsted church: *Ex Italia reverses/inspectis antiquorum aedificiorum Reliquijs Artes Romanus in Patrium transtulit,/Et inter Principes viros qui jam Architecturam /inAnglia restituere et perpolire coeperant/Enituit pene Primus.*

Little is known about Phillips's early life, who in Italy was described as the 'handsome Englishman'. His extensive travels in France and Italy followed his inheritance of Garendon in 1729. He returned to England after Easter 1732, when he was among the first connoisseurs to be elected to the Society of Dilettanti, no doubt due to family relationships, for his mother was a first cousin of Sir Francis Dashwood of West Wycombe.

His surviving album of drawings is precious evidence of his first-hand study of ancient Rome, unlike the architecture of Lord Burlington, derivative from the printed paper evidence of Palladio. What is even more exceptional is his study of the Roman architecture of Provence and Italy, using that architecture to compose his own designs, notably the Arch of Titus in Rome that was only restored in its completeness in 1822. As extraordinary is his record drawing of the Porte du Peyrou at Montpellier and his associated Palladian designs for building around the Place Royale du Peyrou in an English Palladian style, a unique example of English Palladianism in France. The park at Garendon is one of the finest examples of an antique Roman templescape, albeit one of small acreage, although his incomplete Palladian house has been demolished.

41 Ambrose Phillips
'The Garendon Album', c.1730

Bound manuscript
RIBA Drawings Collection

Robert Hampden-Trevor, 4th Baron Trevor and 1st Viscount Hampden (1706–83)

Robert Hampden Trevor, 4th Baron Trevor and 1st Viscount Hampden, was educated at Queen's College, Oxford and was elected a Fellow of All Souls in 1725. Trevor possibly discovered his interest in architecture at Queen's, where from 1710 to 1721 George Clarke and Nicholas Hawksmoor were planning the college. Trevor was a diplomat at The Hague, and from 1759 to 1765 was a joint postmaster general. He was distinguished for his intellectual and literary achievements, and as a connoisseur his collection of drawings and prints was regarded as 'one of the choicest in England'. Although the dozen of his surviving architectural drawings show him to have had great ability in architecture, no building designed by him has been identified, although when he succeeded to the Great Hampden estates in Buckinghamshire in 1754, the Gothic additions at that house must surely be by him. All his drawings betray Baroque tendencies that might suggest a study of Oxford building. Indeed he produced a Pantheon-like rotunda design for the Radcliffe Library c.1737.

42 4th Baron Trevor
Design for a house in Spring Gardens,

Pen, ink & grey wash
RIBA Drawings Collection

Right: Drawing by Ambrose Phillips of the Roman Triumphal Arch at Orange from the Garendon Album (Cat.41)

Below: Design by Ambrose Phillips for the Place Royale du Peyrou, Montpellier, from the Garendon Album (Cat.41)

ESTATE IMPROVERS

John Freeman (c.1689–1752)

With the exception of the saloon in Honington Hall, Warwickshire, built for Joseph Townsend, John Freeman confined his architectural virtuosity to his own estate, at Fawley Court, Bucks., which he inherited in 1707. He has left a substantial number of designs, notably for various garden buildings. The Gothic folly, intended to display classical marbles from the Arundel collection, is an astonishingly advanced building of the Gothic Revival, probably dating to before 1731 when Freeman bought the adjacent Henley Park, where he confessed to 'planting trees, making theatres, and building castles in the air'. The 60 architectural titles in his library were of the standard treatises, but significantly few of the usual English design books such as those by Batty Langley or William Halfpenny. In 1748 Freeman re-fitted the interior of Fawley church from material salvaged from Canons House, Middlesex, when his architect was George Shakespeare. In 1750 he built the family mausoleum in Fawley churchyard, based upon G B Montano's reconstructions of Roman mausolea, which book was in his library. The executant architect for the Honington Hall saloon in 1751 was William Jones.

43 & 44 John Freeman
Designs for a Gothic Temple, c.1728

Pencil (380 x 245)
Private Collection

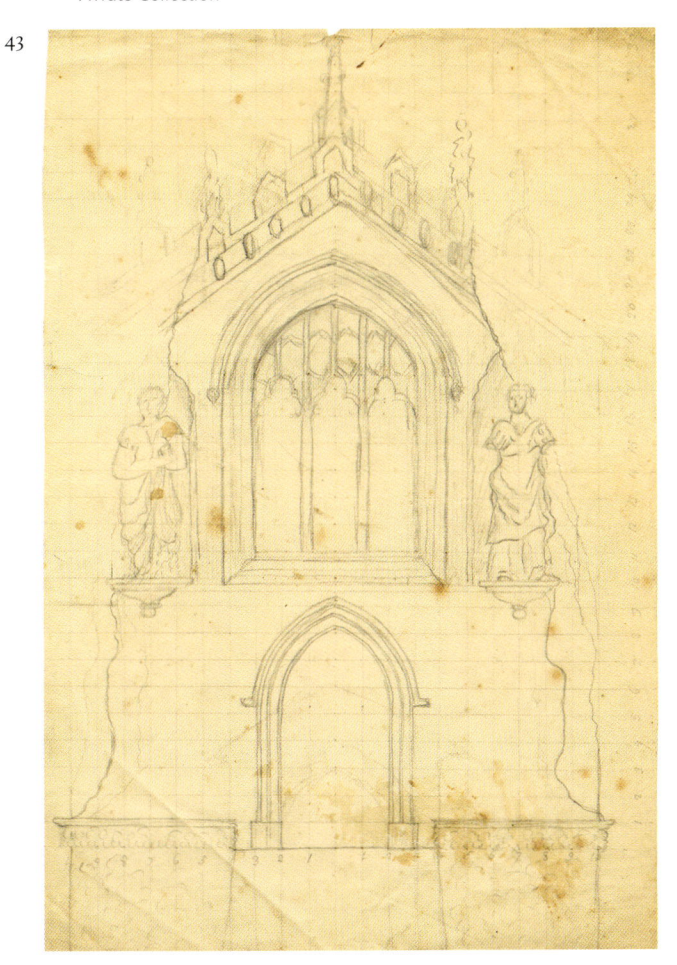

The Gothic Temple at Fawley Court   Photo: Robert Hradsky

45 John Freeman
Design for floor of Gothic Temple, c.1738

Pen & ink (225 x 280)
Private Collection

46–49 John Freeman
Designs for Rustic Bridge, c.1728

Pen (202 x 187; 130 x 300; 193 x 185; 255 x 374)
Private Collection

John Buxton (1685–1731)

The son and heir of Robert Buxton of Channons Hall, John Buxton also inherited the Earsham estate in Norfolk from his mother. His interest in architecture and skill as a designer is attested by a number of surviving drawings in his hand, now at Cambridge University Library. His work included Blixley Hall in Norfolk and his own house at Earsham. In 1721 he moved to Channons, modernizing the house and constructing a new house, Shadwell Lodge.

47 John Buxton
Design for Shadwell Lodge, c.1721

Pen & ink (207 x 326)
The Syndics of Cambridge University Library

Thomas Hope (1769–1831)

If the French had not occupied Holland in 1795, Thomas Hope might not have come to live in London. From his family home near Haarlem he had travelled extensively throughout Europe and the Near East, making fine topographical drawings. In 1799 he bought the Duchess Street house of General Robert Clerk, designed by Robert Adam, and in 1807 the eighteenth-century Deepdene near Dorking. Both houses would be radically transformed. The first architect employed by Hope was C H Tatham, who prepared designs in June 1799 for the Duchess Street Picture Gallery. As one design is inscribed by Hope 'from my own design, afterwards altered with respect to the lights', this possessive comment might suggest that Tatham was not retained, maybe because their tastes in architecture and the presentation of antique sculpture were so similar. Hope's own design for the interior treatment of the gallery is the only surviving evidence for his paper role as an amateur designer. The Deepdene was transformed in 1818–19 and in 1823, the year it was visited by C R Cockerell. The conservative William Atkinson was executant. It was surely Hope and no other who transformed a plain house into one of the triumphs of European Picturesque architecture, as recognized by Cockerell, who thought 'the *genius loci* is remarkably recalled', and concluded, 'Novelty has a vast effect in archtr. We are sick to see the same thing repeated & over again what has been seen anytime these 100 Yrs. The Deepdene attracts in this respect exceeding but if the Pompeian style can be so cultivated as to practice well it may supersede the Templar style in which we have so long worked.' Hope played a crucial role as a connoisseur, notably by his criticisms in 1804 in his *Observations on the Plans and Elevations designed by James Wyatt, Architect, for Downing College, Camb.; in a letter to Francis Annesley, Esq., M.P.*, and even more so by his printed record of the rooms and furnishings of Duchess Street in *Household Furniture and Interior Decoration*, 1807.

Duchess Street was demolished in 1850, and the Deepdene, by British Rail (curse them!), in 1969.

Thomas Wright (1711–86)

Thomas Wright could be regarded as the arch amateur of them all. He was an astronomer, architect and landscape gardener, who even at the age of 14 was, 'much in love with Mathematics' and 'very much given to the amusements of Drawing, Planning of Maps and Building'. As an astronomer he published *Universal Vicissitudes of the Seasons*, 1737, *The Use of the Globes*, 1740, *Clavis Coelestis*, 1742, and *An Original Theory and New Hypothesis of the Universe*, 1750. He is credited with the discovery of the Milky Way. He spent his life travelling through the genealogies of linked families, passing on from one to the other, and often staying for weeks on end. Wherever he went, he advised on and designed, architecture, gardens, and garden buildings, from the earliest, Beaumont Lodge, Old Windsor, for the Dowager, Duchess of Kent, in 1743, to an observatory for himself at Westerton Hill, Durham, a year before his death. The families to which he was closest were those of the Duchess of Kent and her relations at Wrest Park, Bedfordshire; Norborne Berkeley and his sister Elizabeth Berkeley (later 4th Duchess of Beaufort) at Stoke Giffard and Badminton, Gloucestershire, and the 2nd Duke of Halifax. Another friend was the Earl of Limerick, who is associated with his travels in Ireland, 1746–47, when Wright published *Louthiana, or an Introduction to the Antiquities of Ireland*, 1748, a pioneering work. His most significant architectural works included Nuthall Temple, Nottinghamshire, for Sir Charles Sedley 1754, one of the four great Palladian rotunda villas in England; the extensive remodelling of Stoke Giffard; the south front of Horton House, Northants., c.1760, and the building of Hampton Court House, Middlesex, c.1765, for Lord Halifax. But above all Wright is famed for the myriad of ornamental garden buildings, most notably on the Badminton estate. What confuses the historian is the fact that Wright neither appears in building accounts, nor is he paid. Not only did he teach mathematics, the polite arts, drawing, and astronomy to the families, but he was an endearing companion who seems everywhere to have been treated as one of the family. In a sense he is not unlike William Kent, whom he could have met at Badminton in 1747, if not earlier, for Wright's pen and ink landscape studies are almost indistinguishable from those by Kent.

51 Thomas Wright

Plate D from *Six Original Designs of Arbours*, 1755
'Elevation of an Ornithon, or Arbour of the Aviary Kind, chiefly contrived for the Reception of singing and other beautiful Birds'

Engraving (300 x 490)
Private Collection

LADY AMATEURS

Lady Wilbraham (1632–1705)

Elizabeth, later Lady Wilbraham, was the only daughter and heir of Edward Mytton (d.1638) of Weston in Staffordshire to whose estates she succeeded at the age of six. As a 20-year-old, she married Sir Thomas Wilbraham of Woodhey in Cheshire in the parish church of St Andrew at Weston and appears to have demonstrated a headstrong management of her family property as her articulate pose in Sir Peter Lely's portrait might suggest. A silver cup in the church at Acton on her husband's Cheshire estate is inscribed 'The gift of the Honble. Lady Wilbraham of Weston in Staffordshire to the Church of Acton in Cheshire', making no reference to either her husband or their Cheshire property. Her architectural endeavours appear to be poorly documented, although speculation has attributed her involvement at a number of houses without firm evidence. Lady Wilbraham's rebuilding of Weston Park from 1671 and her husband's seat at Woodhey in the 1680s are referred to in the manuscript notes on the flyleaves of her copy of Godfrey Richards's 1663 English translation of Palladio's *First Book of Architecture* which remains in the collection at Weston. Attesting to her knowledge of architecture, the notes record the cost of materials and work. They also include a memorandum of her bargain with Sir William Wilson, the sculptor for setting up four monuments, '2 of the Better, 2 of the Worser, sort and for finding alapaster [sic] and marble £23'.

52 Andrea Palladio
The First Book of Architecture (1st English translation Godfrey Richards), 1663
Printed book
The Weston Park Foundation

This volume contains many contemporary notes in Lady Wilbraham's hand, some relating to the building of Weston Park and the Church at Weston and concerning costs and prices agreed.

Ada (Augusta) King, Countess of Lovelace (1815–52)

Ada (Augusta) King, Countess of Lovelace, was born Ada Byron, the only child of Lord Byron the poet and Anna Isabella Noel Milbanke, so soon to be estranged from her husband. Ada secured initial fame through the opening lines of canto three of Byron's *Childe Harold*:

Ada! Sole daughter of my house and heart?
When last I saw thy young blue eyes they smiled,
And then we parted – not as now we part, But with a hope.

She was deliberately brought up by her mother, fearful of her becoming a poet, as a mathematician and scientist, taught by the famous mathematician Augustus de Morgan. In 1833 aged only 18 she met Charles Babbage, a conjunction of minds that would prove decisive in the history of the computer, because they both worked together on his new calculating engine, she proving a genius in providing clear explanatory texts. She is honoured in the USA by the Department of Defence naming its computer software language Ada.

In 1835 Ada married William King, 8th Baron King of Ockham, created Earl of Lovelace in 1838. Owning estates in North Devon, soon after 1835 on a headland above Porlock Weir she created a rustic Plinean villa overlooking the sea. It was really an earlier *cottage ornée* substantially enlarged, and was notable for the tunnel struck through the cliffs, debouching on to the headland, where the cliffs behind were faced and ornamented with arcuated Roman-style ruins. It is unclear to what extent she was responsible for Lord Lovelace's East Horsley Towers before her tragic death in 1852, when she was buried at her request next to her father.

Below: Sketch of Ashley Combe, Somerset

Sarah Losh (c.1786–1853)

Sara or Sarah Losh was the architect of at least eighteen building works in and around her native village of Wreay in Cumbria. Her masterpiece, the parish church of St Mary, was consecrated in 1842. Built in a style she described as 'modified Saxon or early Lombard', it was designed as a memorial to her sister Catherine. The astonishing iconographic programme expresses a romantic pantheism, its imagery playing on symbols of eternity and resurrection, drawn from pre-Christian sources as well as the natural world. Losh, who was widely read and well-informed about contemporary debates on 'natural theology' and evolution, also incorporated images of fossil ferns in the eastern windows, suggesting their presence at the dawn of Creation.

Losh worked on the church herself, with members of her family and local people. She carved the font. The lectern is by John Scott, made from bog oak, and the building work was undertaken by the mason William Hindson. In its use of individual craftsmen and in the freedom of expression in the carving St Mary's anticipated Ruskin and the Arts and Crafts ideal. It is also a monument to the spirit of an age poised between the Romantics and the Victorians.

Right: Mausoleum in churchyard of St Mary, Wreay. Photo: Gavin Stamp

Below: St Mary, Wreay, view of apse. Photo: Gavin Stamp

THE LUNATIC FRINGE

Some designs by amateurs could be exceedingly odd – the result of an untutored hand and unfettered imagination. There is more than a little lunacy in Bunny Hall, the strange Baroque house built by the wrestling parson Sir Thomas Parkyns in Nottinghamshire in 1723; and Lord Holland designed Kingsgate on wildly grand scale, surrounding it by a park and buildings drawn from the realms of pure fantasy.

Sir Thomas Parkyns (1662–1741)

Among the many talents of Sir Thomas Parkyns that included the 'ability to throw a tenant, combat a paradox, quote Martial or sign a mittimus with any man of his own age or county', was architecture. A competent mathematician, with a knowledge of hydraulics and engineering, Parkyns was able at 'Contriving & Drawing all his Plomns without an Architect'. The inscription on his monument in Bunny church records that he 'Built the Schoolhouse and Hospital . . . the Mannor Houses in Bunney and East Leake . . . the Vicaridge House & most of the Farm Houses in Bunney and Bradmore.' Bunny Hall, dated 1723, is one of the most eccentric houses in Britain, its front with a huge armorial achievement clasped by four whacky giant Ionic pilasters. It has quite rightly been described as 'belonging to the lunatic fringe of the Baroque', but it shares with the almshouses in the village a flavour of Low Countries Baroque. As the author of *The Inn-Play, or, Cornish-Hugg Wrestler*, 1727, dedicated to George II, Parkyns not only recommends wrestling as fostering military strength against the French, but also hopes that Parliament 'will establish a stage in every market-town at which gentlemen wearing swords can settle their affronts at single-stick'. The annual wrestling competition at Bunny lasted from 1712 until 1810.

Thomas Wynn, 1st Baron Newborough (1736–1807)

Thomas Wynn, 1st Baron Newborough, of Glynlliffon, Caernarvonshire, first travelled to Italy in 1759–60 where he is recorded as studying at the Turin Academy in 1759 with Thomas Robinson, Baron Grantham. In 1762 he designed the spectacular house on the cliffs at Kingsgate, Kent, for Henry Fox, later Lord Holland, said to be a re-creation of Cicero's Formian villa at Baiae, although this was a literary comparison. It was certainly a reconstruction of Pliny's Laurentian villa. Its vast façade was 260 feet in length with a huge hexastyle Doric portico opening to a vast neo-classical hall and two courtyards. In 1767 Holland wrote to his wife that 'The back part of the House looks now just like a Villa as I meant.' There were 8 major rooms including a Saloon of Neptune. Initially Newborough had the assistance of John Vardy as executant. By 1782 Newborough had gone broke owing to an obsession with the Caernarvon Militia, fears of a French invasion, and the building at his expense of Forts Belan and Williamsburg on the Menai Straits. In order to avoid creditors, in 1782 he fled to Italy with his wife, who died in Leghorn, and his son, 'who was allowed to run wild'. He caused consternation when he married Stella Chiappini, an 'Italian singing girl about 13 years old', described as 'wilder than a colt', but who in rebuff described him as a 'stout old grey beard, from behind whose few and discoloured teeth came forth an offensive breath'. She married him in 1786, assuming the title of Countess. On his return to England he designed the classical Temple of Friendship for Charles James Fox at St Anne's Hill, Surrey, and may then have dotted the Kingsgate cliff-top with the most extraordinary and bizarre collection of follies, including the Convent of St Mildrid, a 'Tower built on the Highest spot in the Island in memory of Robert Whitfield Esq', a Tower dedicated to 'Thomas Harley, Ld Mayor of London, 1768', Countess's Fort, and one titled 'The Ornament and (under Thomas Wynn Esq) the Adorner of Kingsgate', all engraved in bistre by Basire.

53 Thomas Wynn (engraved by Basire)
Kingsgate elevation and plan, 1768
Engraving (330 × 495)
Private Collection

54–56 Thomas Wynn (engraved by Basire)
Designs for monuments, Kingsgate, Kent, 1768
Bistre engravings, (300 × 323; 340 × 245; 310 × 245)
Private Collection

Left: Bunny Hall, Nottinghamshire, by Sir Thomas Parkyns 'one of the most eccentric houses in Britain'. © Crown copyright.NMR

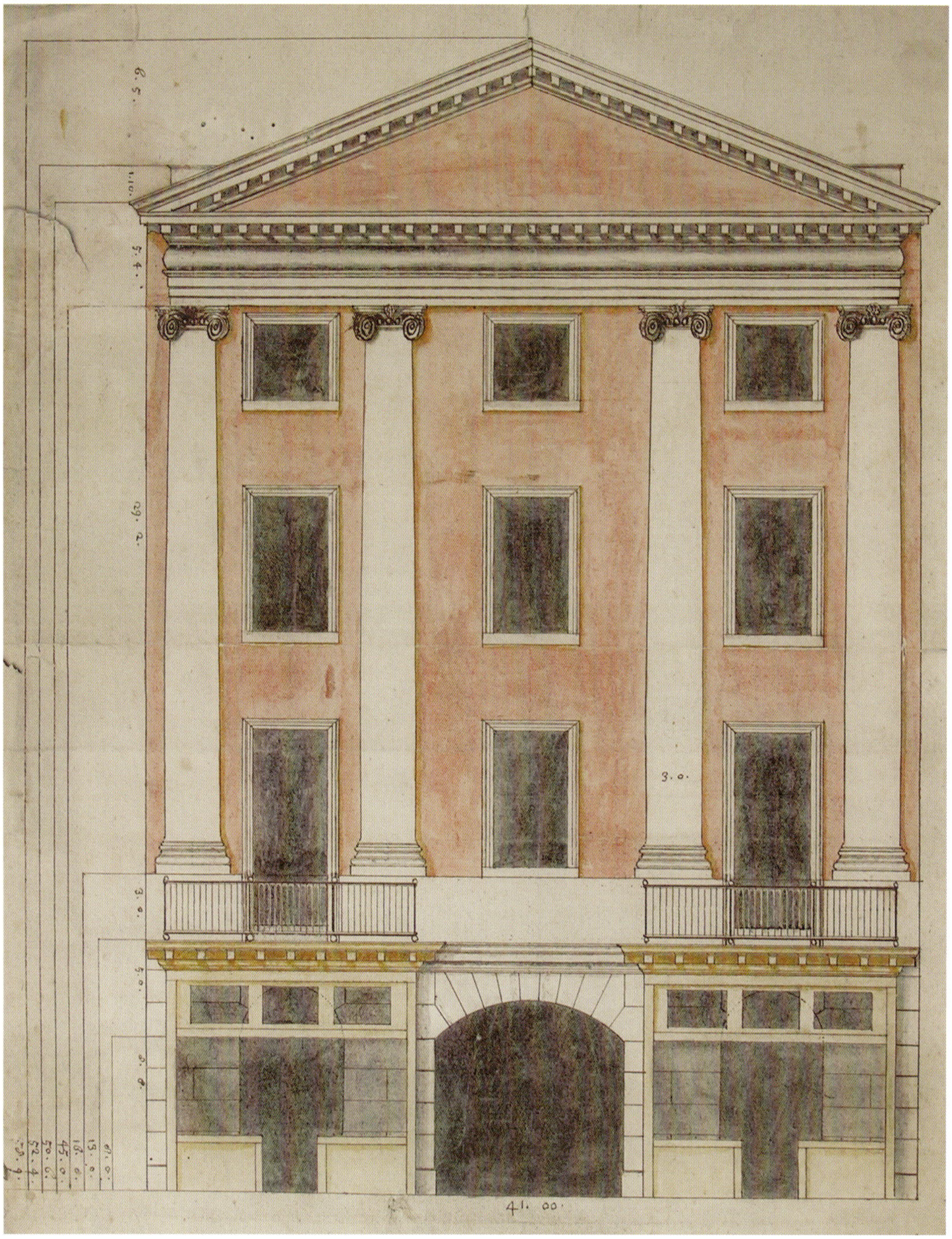

7